insight text guide

Sue Sherman

Rainbow's End

Jane Harrison

First published in 2022, reprinted in 2023, 2024, 2025, 2026.

Insight Publications Pty Ltd
3/350 Charman Road
Cheltenham VIC 3192
Australia
Tel: +61 3 8571 4950
Email: books@insightpublications.com.au

www.insightpublications.com.au

A catalogue record for this book is available from the National Library of Australia

Jane Harrison's Rainbow's End / Sue Sherman

Sue Sherman asserts the moral right to be identified as the author of this work.

ISBNs:
9781922771117 (print)
9781922771124 (digital)

Cover design by Melisa Paredes

Proudly Printed in Australia by Ligare Book Printers

contents

CHARACTER MAP

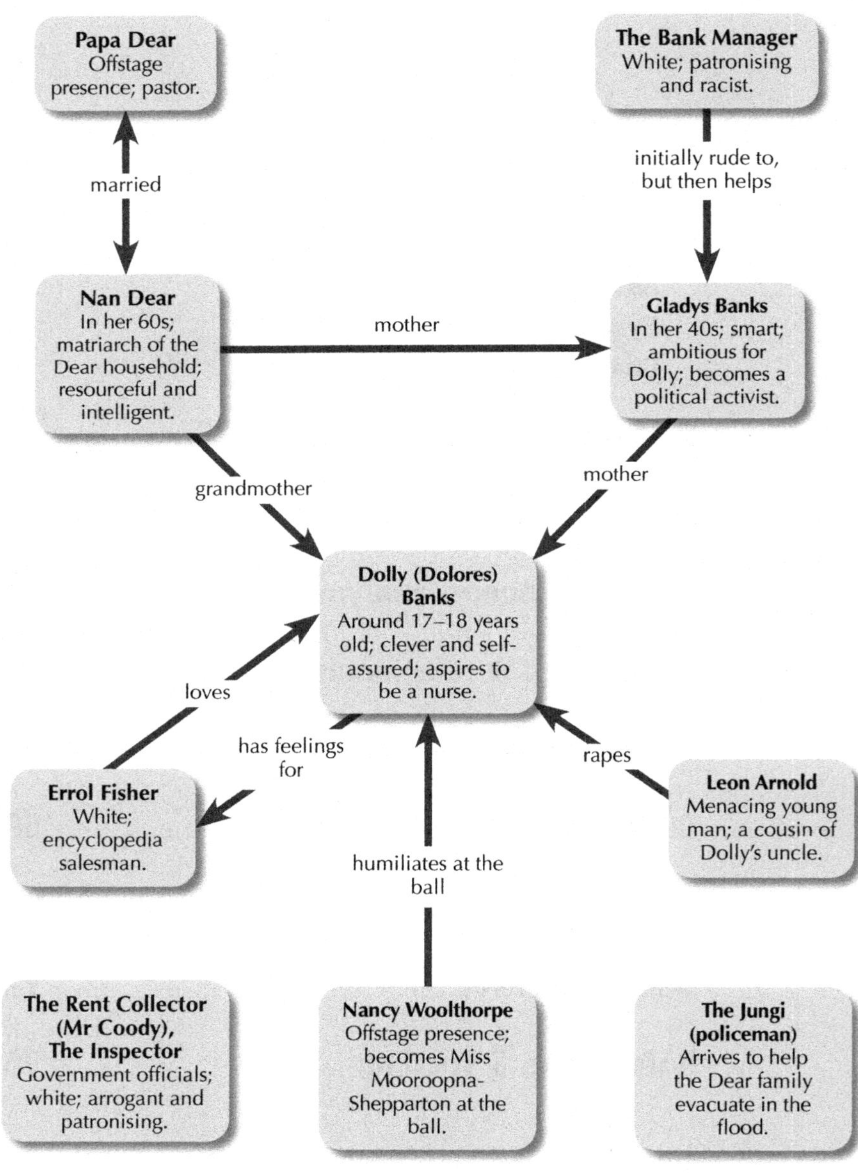

OVERVIEW

About the author

A descendant of the Muruwari people (from the Bourke and Brewarrina areas), Jane Harrison is a playwright, critic and novelist. Harrison worked first as a copywriter for advertising agencies and, after being laid off from her copywriting job, she joined the Ilbijerri Theatre Company as a writer, seeing it as an opportunity to work with a new creative form and, more importantly, to incorporate her heritage into her work. She was commissioned to write the play *Stolen* (2000), which was subsequently included for study in VCE English and the NSW HSC syllabus. The recipient of the Kate Challis RAKA Award in 2002, *Stolen* remains Harrison's best-known and most widely toured play. In 2014, her debut novel *Becoming Kirrali Lewis* was shortlisted for the Prime Minister's Literary Awards and the Victorian Premier's Award.

Harrison also holds a Master of Arts degree from the Queensland University of Technology for a thesis about the challenges facing non-Aboriginal theatre practitioners when they tell First Nations stories. In an interview for ABC.net, Harrison explained:

> The whole issue of identity, it's what I feel when I'm with my people. It's a strong sense of belonging that is kind of deep. I get very fired up about issues. I'm not a terribly political person but I feel a very strong emotional connection to those issues. I want to do my little bit to help educate people and to help people acknowledge that history. (Jane Harrison, cited in Encyclopedia.com 2019)

Although she describes herself as not 'terribly political', Harrison's awareness of identity politics is evident in her interview on the *Garret* podcast. As a child, she had 'always loved books' but was disappointed by the absence of Aboriginal characters. The closest her childhood reading material ever came to an Aboriginal character was in Arthur Upfield's 'Bony' books with Detective-Inspector Napoleon Bonaparte (Bony); yet there were 'no Aboriginal novels based in cities or metropolitan settings'. Thus, growing up in a city, and with her Indigenous* Australian lineage, Harrison never saw herself 'reflected' in Australian literature, and she wanted to write something that reflected some of her own experiences (Edwards 2015). In writing *Rainbow's End* (2007), Harrison felt fortunate in being able to draw on Aboriginal Australian Elders' reminiscences about life on The Flats and the establishment of Rumbalara (the First Nations people's housing estate at Mooroopna, p.121), and she unequivocally condemns the substandard housing provided for First Nations families in the 1950s.

The play also recalls the historical tragedy of Indigenous children forcibly removed from their families which, even today, resonates painfully throughout Aboriginal communities. This is certainly the case for Nan and Gladys in *Rainbow's End*. Through Nan's stories and Gladys' political awakening, Harrison tells the story of her people's dispossession and oppression, but she also celebrates their resilience. In a Q&A blog on the Readings website (Lehman 2015), Harrison expresses regret that, while Aboriginal histories, stories and characters are part of our shared history, there are so few of these stories in popular culture. As a writer herself, she considers that her 'first responsibility is to Aboriginal readers or audience'. Thus she regards herself as 'a conduit for telling stories' about their 'lives and experiences', and also wants to share these stories more broadly. Fiction, Harrison explains, is 'an important way' for First Nations people 'to have a voice' (Lehman 2015). She believes that her plays, in particular, allow her to get those stories 'into the hands of as many people' as she can (Edwards 2015).

---

*We acknowledge that all terms used to describe Aboriginal and Torres Strait Islander peoples have limitations, but in this guide we have chosen to use the terms 'Indigenous', 'First Nations' and 'Aboriginal', and do so with respect.

Synopsis

Nan Dear, her daughter Gladys Banks and Gladys' daughter Dolly live in a humpy (a small and shabby hut) on 'The Flats': a flood-prone First Nations housing settlement near Shepparton, Victoria. Life is difficult, filled with mishaps and catastrophes ranging from Gladys' failed attempt to see the Queen, to the shocking sexual assault on Dolly, to disastrous floods that damage and, eventually, destroy the family's home and most of their possessions. Yet there are also positive moments: Errol's (accidental) visit to the Dear family to sell encyclopedia subscriptions results in Gladys signing up for a subscription to *Encyclopedia Britannica,* at least partially as a means to encourage his obvious interest in Dolly (p.146). Dolly attends a ball with Errol and, in a fit of jealous spite, Nancy Woolthorpe, a vindictive white girl, humiliates Dolly by loudly announcing that her dress is made from old curtains that the Woolthorpes had dumped at the tip (p.166). Utterly distraught, Dolly rushes out of the room, and Leon, one of Dolly's cousins, tries to force himself on her. When Errol defends her, Leon attacks and injures him. Later that evening Leon sexually assaults her and she becomes pregnant.

After a devastating second flood, the people from The Flats are unwillingly relocated to a new Aboriginal cooperative: Rumbalara. The concrete houses are drab and unwelcoming, and a petition is drawn up by Gladys and Papa Dear, on behalf of the Indigenous Australian residents, demanding more suitable living conditions. When Papa Dear (who has been delayed at a funeral, p.196) fails to arrive to speak at the meeting, Gladys steps up, delivering a stirring speech demanding appropriate housing, greater employment opportunities and social justice for First Nations people (pp.196–8). Even in 2005, when the play was first performed, many of these goals had not been achieved. Despite this, the hope of a better future for First Nations people is conveyed by Dolly's nursing scholarship, the birth of her child and the happy prospect of Dolly and Errol's wedding.

Character summaries

Dolly (Dolores) Banks

A seventeen/eighteen-year-old Aboriginal Australian, Dolly is a self-assured, clever and pretty teenager. When she meets Errol 'an instant spark of attraction' passes between them (p.132). Dolly is a high-achieving student and would like to become a nurse (p.142).

Gladys Banks

Dolly's mother is in her forties and, at the beginning of the play, is an enthusiastic royalist who is excited about the visit of Queen Elizabeth. She later becomes a passionate advocate for First Nations people's rights.

Nan Dear

Gladys' mother and Dolly's grandmother, who is in her sixties, disapproves of royalty and of Gladys' obsession with it. An energetic and outspoken woman, Nan rules the household.

Errol Fisher

Errol is a nervous and awkward young white man trying to sell encyclopedia subscriptions. He and Dolly fall in love and eventually marry.

Papa Dear

Papa Dear is Nan's husband but is not Gladys' father. He and Gladys are unaware of this and Nan would prefer that they did not know. A travelling pastor and a political activist, Papa Dear is mostly absent from home.

The Inspector

The Inspector is an ignorant, arrogant and patronising government official who believes that 'the Aborigine needs to be absorbed into the community' and should learn to 'live like us' (p.152).

The Bank Manager

The Bank Manager is another condescending and arrogant man. He responds to Gladys' enquiry about a teller's position for Dolly by querying Dolly's capacity, as an Aboriginal Australian, to 'fit in' at the bank (p.163). However, he does eventually agree to put Dolly on the list for an interview.

Nancy Woolthorpe

Nancy, a privileged white girl, deliberately humiliates Dolly at the ball by announcing, for all to hear, that Dolly's dress is made from curtains that Nancy's family had dumped at the tip (p.166).

Leon Arnold

Dolly's roughneck cousin Leon fancies her; he gets drunk and tries to assault her ouside the ball (pp.166–7). He also physically assaults Errol, who intervenes to protect Dolly. Leon later rapes Dolly, leaving her pregnant.

The Jungi

The policeman comes to help Nan and Gladys evacuate their belongings to higher ground but, on Gladys' urging, walks away to help another family, leaving the encyclopedias on the ground (pp.174–5).

The Rent Collector (Mr Coody)

The Rent Collector is another arrogant and patronising government official; he informs Nan that, because of Dolly's pregnancy, their house is not 'suitable' for the 'extended family' (p.185).

BACKGROUND & CONTEXT

Historical context

The colonisation of Australia by British forces, beginning with the arrival of the First Fleet in 1788, had a devastating impact on First Nations Australians. One reason for this was that Indigenous Australian peoples had no immunity from introduced diseases, and many died as a result. A further and even more shocking factor was the brutal slaughter of hundreds of First Nations peoples in what became known as the Frontier Wars: this was the systematic massacre of First Nations people defending their territory against armed British soldiers and settlers who considered the land to be theirs for the taking. These massacres were supported by colonial governments and sometimes involved government forces (Allam & Evershed 2019).

The attempted eradication of First Nations peoples and their culture remained Australian government policy throughout much of the twentieth century. The focus of these policies was on assimilating children, who were considered more capable of adapting to white society than adults were. Children were forcibly removed from their parents and their communities; they were instructed to reject their heritage and forced to conform to white cultural norms. In severing the children's connections with their family and culture, authorities often changed the children's names and forbade them to speak their own language. Some children were adopted by white families and were often physically abused and treated as unpaid servants. In *Rainbow's End*, Gladys' experience in domestic service is the reason she lacks a formal education, which in turn leads to her obsession with Dolly's education as well as her own determination to learn to read and write.

Writing as political activism

Indigenous Australian artists such as Jane Harrison have claimed public performance spaces to showcase First Nations history, culture and resilience. Maryrose Casey and Cathy Craigie have summarised the central role of theatre for Indigenous writers and performers:

> In the 1960s and 1970s, when Indigenous theatrical works occupied a prominent place on Australian stages, writers and performers created work that blended Aboriginal performance traditions with European stage conventions in both form and content. Traditional Indigenous performance works alternate rhythmically between speech and silence, between the past and the present and between performance and story. Within these innovations of form, writers such as Kevin Gilbert, Robert Merritt and Jack Davis individually and collectively brought contemporary Indigenous stories into the foreground of Australian mainstream culture. (Casey & Craigie 2006)

Indigenous women playwrights have also made significant contributions. Eva Johnson's plays in the 1980s and 1990s focused on Aboriginal Australians' struggle to overcome colonial oppression, while Jane Harrison's *Stolen* (first performed in 1998) introduced many non-Indigenous audiences to the experiences of the Stolen Generations. Some playwrights created single-actor plays in which the performer directly addresses the audience: examples include Wesley Enoch and Deborah Mailman's *The 7 Stages of Grieving* (1996) and Leah Purcell's *Box the Pony* (1997). Indigenous theatre tells 'individual and collective stories' using elements such as 'music and song, shifts in style and time and the use of Aboriginal languages' (Casey & Craigie 2006), elements that are also evident in *Rainbow's End*.

With public performances of her plays, Jane Harrison has also condemned the impact of government policies on First Nations

Australian women and children and emphatically situated herself within a strong tradition of politically active Indigenous Australian playwrights. Such strong activism has been driven by a need for recompense and reconciliation. Another significant issue has been the legal recognition of Native Title. This resulted in the establishment of a National Native Title Tribunal to register, hear and determine Native Title claims. The subsequent legislation has been part of a journey towards reconciliation, designed to help non-Indigenous Australians 'understand and accept the wrongs of the past' and ensure that they are 'never repeated' (Reconciliation Australia 2020).

Also important in this regard have been plays with sympathetically constructed Indigenous Australian characters, while the use of domestic and recognisable settings have helped to make political and historical issues more accessible to non-Indigenous audiences, as is clearly the case in *Rainbow's End*. Yet the play also shows Harrison's frustration with governments whose political rhetoric has not been followed by appropriate action, leaving First Nations Australians in the 1950s (and even in the twenty-first century) without the same basic human rights as non-Indigenous Australians.

The Flats and Cummeragunja

Cummeragunja embodies the notion of home for Nan. Established in 1888 on the NSW side of the Murray River on Yorta Yorta/Bangerang Country, Cummeragunja became home to many Aboriginal people. Initially it was a successful farm where Aboriginal workers sought to be self-sufficient. In 1915, however, life at Cummeragunja changed drastically. The New South Wales Protection Board 'took greater control'; those who worked were given 'inadequate and unhealthy rations' and any funds raised 'went to the Board' (ABC et al. 2004). By the 1930s conditions had deteriorated and illnesses such as tuberculosis were sweeping through the station. In 1939 the residents decided to take a stand and the first mass strike of Aboriginal people occurred.

Many of those who left Cummeragunja in the 1939 walk-off found new homes on The Flats, on the Goulburn River flood plain between Mooroopna and Shepparton. By the early 1950s 'it was believed that the numbers had grown to approximately 300 people' (River Connect 2011). Neville Atkinson, a Bangerang man, describes humpies constructed out of 'flattened kero tins' and the families' exposure to extremes of heat and cold. Nevertheless, 'our community was able to continue our cultural heritage to some extent. These camps were poor, but they were orderly and organised' (Atkinson 2006).

GENRE, STRUCTURE & LANGUAGE

The word *drama* was originally a Greek word meaning 'to do'. Thus, drama (as a public event) is always associated with such concepts as 'performance', 'action', 'actors' and 'stage'.

Genre

Drama has a number of generic features; these are used by the playwright to explore ideas and to position the audience to respond to characters and events in particular ways. The following list explains the main generic features and indicates some of the ways in which Jane Harrison uses them in *Rainbow's End*.

Plot: the basic storyline of the play.

Theme: a central idea explored in the play. In *Rainbow's End*, the main theme is the damaging effects on First Nations peoples of Britain's colonisation of Australia.

Characters: fictional persons created by authors to convey ideas and viewpoints. Characters also embody the values that playwrights endorse or condemn.

Dialogue: words written by the playwright and spoken by the characters. Characters' language choices, speech patterns and lexicon (wider vocabulary) reveal aspects of their identities. In this play there are also lines not spoken by the characters onstage, but played from recordings. For example, the frequent background sound of radio broadcasts is a form of dialogue. The quiz show *Pick-A-Box* emphasises Gladys' broad general knowledge, while the radio commentary on the Queen's visit connects listeners like Gladys to the glamorous world of celebrity royalty. In contrast, the fade-out of the royal visit broadcast when Nan enters (p.124) signifies her disapproval of the monarchy. Also evident is the way these broadcasts promote the values of a white-centred world.

Setting: where (and sometimes when) the action takes place. In *Rainbow's End,* the main setting is the interior of the Dears' ramshackle humpy. It reveals their poverty but also their resilience and their love of home and family.

Spectacle: the visual elements of a play, including sets, costumes and special effects. In Harrison's play, theatrical elements such as settings, props and costumes have symbolic significance.

- ***Costume*** elements in this play include Gladys' borrowed high heels in which she walks for several hours, hoping to catch a glimpse of the Queen. She also wears white gloves, emulating the British monarch and tacitly endorsing Britain's cultural superiority. Dolly's ball gown, on the other hand, celebrates the transformation of discarded curtains into a glamorous dress, contrasting Nan's skill and resourcefulness with the wastefulness of many white Australians.
- ***Props*** include encyclopedias offering knowledge – and perhaps enhancing career opportunities for Dolly – and magazines (with their trivial content), often providing distraction from the hardships of life. These props also symbolise an Anglocentric culture that marginalises First Nations Australians. Laundry items, similarly, promote the desirability of whiteness and cleanliness – the imagery of whiteness pervades the play and carries racist connotations.
- Various types of ***staging effects*** symbolise ideas in the play. ***Lighting*** changes can indicate a time change and also (symbolically) foreshadow danger; for example, the darkness when Nan's lamp is extinguished (p.168) emphasises Dolly's isolation and vulnerability, and evokes the lurking presence of Leon. Other dramatic visual effects are displayed in the twice-flooded interior of the Dears' humpy, with its sodden walls and ruined household items. This image implicitly condemns the government's allocation of a flood plain for Aboriginal people's housing (p.124, pp.173–5).

Performance elements: these include aspects of vocal expression such as pitch, pace, pauses and tone. They can carry symbolic significance and provide deeper insight into the main themes of the play. Examples include the following.

- When Gladys steps up to deliver the petition (p.197), the pause when she 'looks at the piece of paper wildly' causes a 'sustained moment of tension'. The fact that she rises to the challenge suggests her triumph over the adversity of being a 'stolen child' who was denied a proper education.
- The ironic tone of Nan's reference to US President Franklin Roosevelt's 1933 humanitarian economic reforms highlights the inadequacy of the Rumbalara housing development (p.178).
- The Inspector's bureaucratic language and officious tone (p.152) highlight the government's attempt to disguise racist policies with euphemistic terminology. Telling the family that policies are to help 'ease you into the township' sounds less threatening than the word 'assimilation', which itself is a form of language that hides the concept of genocide.
- Nonverbal expression includes gestures, body language and facial expression. Nan's 'glowering' (glaring, p.134) shows her distrust of interfering white male intruders.
- Stage directions, including those describing aspects of the actors' appearance, delivery or movement, usually convey deeper meaning. Gladys' aptitude with an axe (p.177) metaphorically foreshadows her fierce political activism.

Structure

Rainbow's End begins in medias res (in the middle of the action), abruptly plunging the audience into a crisis point: a time immediately after a flood. Beginning with a prologue, followed by Scenes One and Two divided into parts A and B, and with most of the scenes having a title, the play's structure is somewhat unconventional. The first scene, with its division into parts A and B, is quite fragmented and might reflect a lack of order and control in the Indigenous characters' lives, living in a racist society and housed on a flood plain. In addition, dream sequences frequently disrupt the continuity of the narrative, while the juxtapositions of comforting dreams and uncomfortable reality initially suggest the unattainability of Gladys' and Dolly's hopes and aspirations.

The play is structured around two narrative threads: Gladys' political awakening and Dolly and Errol's romance. Each story has a dramatic climax, with an epiphany (a sudden moment of self-awareness). When Dolly tells Gladys to 'fix' her own house, something in Gladys 'snaps' and she confronts the councillors at the meeting (p.179). Similarly, when Errol promises Dolly a 'better life', she recognises his assumption of white racial superiority and ends their relationship (p.172).

The subsequent action of the play, however, moves towards a satisfactory resolution for each narrative, culminating in Gladys' stirring 'petition' speech (pp.196–8) and Nan's dream sequence of Dolly and Errol's wedding (p.198). Significantly, the larger issue of Aboriginal housing is left unresolved.

The song 'Que Sera, Sera', strategically placed at the opening and closing of the play, initially portrays the government's laissez-faire attitude (allowing things to remain as they are) while at the play's end, the song might augur change for the better.

Language

The characters' language reflects their personalities and is often indicative of their gender, race and class. The voice of the playwright is conveyed through her characters' language, which reveals their (and Harrison's) values.

Nan is opinionated and straight-talking. For example, when informing Gladys that she 'won't be needing any of them encyclops' (encyclopedias, p.136), Nan is scornfully dismissive of their relevance to her family's circumstances. Nan's vernacular (colloquial speech) reveals her lack of education, which in turn emphasises her lower-class status. This is characteristic of First Nations Australians of her generation who were denied an education. Nan's language also adds a comic touch to the play. Her humour is ironic; the advice she offers Gladys (who is dressing up to see the Queen) is gently mocking – Gladys picks beans for a living (p.124) and, with or without white gloves, it is very unlikely that she will be noticed by the Queen.

Dolly is honest and assertive, particularly regarding racial discrimination. She calls out Errol when he refers to Indigenous Australians as 'you people' (p.141), thus categorising them as 'the other', and for assuming that his world is better than hers (p.172). She confronts her mother as well, accusing her of wanting Dolly to be like the white girls (p.158), thus forcing Gladys to recognise her own feelings of racial inferiority: 'You're always telling me to stick up for myself, but when do you, eh?' (p.162). As Gladys explains to Errol: 'She's a Dear, and us Dears are well known for being straight talkers' (p.190). As an affirmation of her cultural heritage, Dolly also uses Indigenous vernacular and a '*blackfella accent*' when she threatens to kick Ester's boys 'up the moom' (p.137) and when she introduces Errol to the taste of 'snooty goggles' (p.147). She is fluent and articulate when she explains to Errol that she wouldn't trade places with Nancy 'for anything' because she is perfectly happy to stay with 'my mum and my nan' (p.172).

Errol's awkward and halting language shows his nervousness and insecurity. He seems so inept as a salesman that he needs Dolly's help with his sales pitch (p.133), and might initially be seen as comic relief, though his verbal blunders also offend Dolly. When he remarks that the glass of water she brings him is 'made out of a can' (p.140), he unintentionally humiliates her. Errol is initially unaware of his politically loaded language, such as his reference to 'you people' (p.140).

Errol's blunders suggest a greater need for sensitivity to the political implications of language in dialogue with First Nations Australians, who have endured many years of racist and condescending language.

At the Rodney Shire meeting **Gladys** becomes the militant voice of ordinary Indigenous Australian people who have had enough of white politicians' procrastination. The voice of Harrison herself is echoed in Gladys' fighting words, particularly in her final fiery speech.

The language of **the Queen** is aloof and formal. Her reference to 'the birthplace of the nation' celebrates colonisation and dismisses 65 000 years of Indigenous Australian civilisation, while her comment about standing 'at last' among Australians refers solely to white Australians (p.124). The Queen's non-inclusive language reflects the non-inclusive attitudes of her white Australian subjects towards First Nations Australians.

The Duke (the Duke of Edinburgh, more commonly known as Prince Philip) was renowned for making spontaneous and often inappropriate remarks. His question 'Where's Father?' (p.127) provides a glimpse of his unconventional personality, and perhaps his need to occasionally liberate himself from the constraints of his official role.

The radio announcer's reference to Indigenous Australians is oblique and insulting. The 'royal couple' is reminded that 'they were in Australia' with a demonstration of 'how to throw a boomerang' (p.128). This tactlessly transforms an element of First Nations culture into a novelty item for the royal couple's entertainment. The announcer's comment that (the boomerang) 'really does come back' (p.128) is patronising in its dismissiveness of Indigenous Australians' expertise with this sophisticated weaponry.

Language is also instructive in **stage directions**. For example, the vulnerability of people living on The Flats is evident in Harrison's descriptions of the waterlogged, mud-spattered interior of the Dear family's humpy, which emphasises their poverty and their powerlessness (p.123, p.176).

Irony is used throughout the play. Verbal irony, when the literal meaning of what is said is the opposite of what is meant, is often a feature of the banter between Nan, Gladys and Dolly. For example, Nan declares that the meeting between the Queen and Papa Dear is a reflection of how important the Queen is – 'getting a meeting with the busiest Aboriginal around!' (p.128) – when it really reflects Papa Dear's importance. Situational irony is evident when the audience learns that Papa Dear is not Gladys' biological father, a fact that Gladys remains unaware of. It is also a feature of early exchanges between Dolly and Errol; for instance, she understands (and the audience can anticipate) the difficulties that might face them if they go to the ball together – 'Do you have any idea what'll happen if you walk into that dance with me?' – but Errol is oblivious: 'Is there some other bloke on the scene?' (p.148).

A more bitter irony is Papa Dear's adherence to Christianity, with its central tenet of the need to 'love one another' – a tenet that is apparently not applicable to white attitudes to First Nations Australians in the 1950s.

The **play's title** draws on legends about pots of gold buried at the ends of rainbows, originating from the invasion of Ireland by Vikings (around 795 AD), who stole and buried gold and other treasures. The Vikings eventually departed, supposedly leaving buried treasure at the ends of rainbows. As a **metaphor,** this suggests the improbability of a brighter future for Harrison's First Nations' characters, because actual rainbows are optical illusions, and they are circular: half-hidden by the horizon, they have no end, and there is no pot of gold.

Another pertinent **allusion** is to the song 'Somewhere Over the Rainbow' from *The Wizard of Oz*. With its yearning for home and a comforting assurance that 'somewhere over the rainbow ... the dreams that you dare to dream really do come true', the song has a poignant resonance for dispossessed First Nations people.

SCENE-BY-SCENE ANALYSIS

ACT ONE

Prologue: Aftermath (p.123)

Summary: *Dolly arrives home from school to find the floor covered with muddy water, and her mother and grandmother using pages from her treasured magazines to cover the wet hessian walls.*

Dolly's disappointment over her ruined magazines is overcome by the urgency of repairing the damaged walls. On a deeper level, the ruin of something precious to her by a destructive flood might be symbolic of British colonisation and its catastrophic impact on First Nations peoples.

Key point

The words 'que sera, sera' (meaning 'whatever will be, will be') describe an attitude called 'cheerful fatalism': a belief that all events are determined in advance, and that human beings are powerless to determine their future.

Key vocabulary

Hessian (p.123): strong, rough fabric made from hemp or stems of tropical plants.

Humpy (p.123): tumbledown shack.

'Que Sera, Sera' (p.123): first published in 1955, the song has three verses progressing through the life of the narrator – from childhood, through young adulthood and parenthood.

Q Is it better to have hopeful dreams, or to resign oneself to an unpromising future? What does Harrison suggest? Explain your reasoning with reference to the text.

Scene One (A): The Queen's Visit (pp.124–7)

Summary: *It is 1954. The scene opens with a radio broadcast of Queen Elizabeth's tour of Australia. All dressed up to get a 'squiz' at the Queen, Gladys wants to have a moment she will remember.*

Gladys' loyalty to the Queen seems more connected with the celebrity status of a 'pretty young monarch' (p.124). Gladys also wants to make her own insignificant life more relevant by connecting it with a historic moment. Nan's reluctance to talk about her family tree (p.125) indicates painful memories. We later learn that Nan was '[taken] advantage of' by a white man who left her pregnant with Gladys (p.187), and Gladys was taken away as a child to be 'assimilated' (p.154).

Key point

Vast sums of government money are spent on celebrating a descendant of the imperialist monarch, in whose name First Nations peoples were stripped of their lands, their cultural heritage and their human rights.

Key vocabulary

Buka bung stew (p.126): stew made from nettles (native plant covered with stinging filaments).

Cummeragunja (p.126): Cummeragunja Station was an Aboriginal reserve; it is likely that Nan's comment references the 1939 walk-off by around 200 Aboriginal Australians in protest against inadequate living conditions and incompetent management.

Flounces (p.124): takes offence at something and walks indignantly away.

Hullaballoo (p.124): a great deal of noise and fuss.

Not ... for all the tea in China (p.124): an expression of refusal to do something, no matter what extravagant inducement is offered.

Scene One (B) (pp.127–8)

Summary: *Gladys walks almost six kilometres in uncomfortable high heels to get a glimpse of the Queen but can't get through the hessian-draped temporary fences alongside the roads.*

While Papa Dear is away on a 'mission to make things better for Aboriginal people', Nan and Gladys put food on the table and Dolly stokes the fire (p.128). In providing sustenance and warmth – the basic necessities of life – these characters embody the strength of women who hold families and communities together when men are absent.

Key point

Items of Gladys' attire reflect her values; the white gloves and white shoes she wears, and her plan to get a taxi so her shoes won't get dirty, might suggest a leaning towards the ways of white people. This might be combined with subconscious feelings of inferiority about the colour of her skin in a racist, postcolonial society.

Key vocabulary

Gallivanting (p.128): going out with the intention of having fun.

Get off your high horse (p.128): stop behaving as though you're superior to everyone else.

Highfalutin' (highfaluting, p.128): pretentious; attempting to impress people.

Q If a vote was held today on whether Australia should become a republic, which way would you vote, and why?

Scene Two (A): Oh, Errol (pp.129–32)

Summary: Pick-A-Box *is on the radio while Gladys chops wood and correctly answers the quiz questions. Dolly urges her mother to go on the show and, in a dream sequence, she imagines Gladys winning a mink stole and a fancy sewing machine.*

Nan is concerned for Dolly's future and (rightly, as it turns out) wary of Leon Arnold, who has 'a wild look' (p.131). Gladys, who was deprived of higher education because of her Aboriginality, constantly reminds Dolly of the importance of education.

Key point

Through references to Ester and her family, Harrison acknowledges the occurrence of family violence in Indigenous Australian communities but the play situates the issue within the historical context of colonisation. This reflects current understandings, which see colonisation, racism and dispossession as some of the underlying causes of the family violence experienced by Aboriginal and Torres Strait Islander women.

Key vocabulary

Bodgies and widgies (p.130): teenage boys and girls who belonged to a rebellious youth subculture in Australia in the 1950s.

Flash Yanks (p.131): loud and showy Americans.

House of Biba (p.130): a London fashion store.

Mink stole (p.130): an expensive fur shoulder wrap worn by women on formal occasions.

Scene Two (B) (pp.132–8)

Summary: *An incompetent encyclopedia salesman, Errol, gets lost in the bush; he sees Gladys at the clothesline and she invites him inside. He embarks on his sales pitch but needs Gladys' help to get through it. When Gladys shows interest, he promptly signs her up for a subscription.*

When Dolly goes outside with Errol, Nan orders Gladys to 'call her back' (p.136). Nan 'watches them suspiciously' from the window (p.136), and later warns Dolly that it is difficult to tell 'a good man from a bad' (p.138). Nan's over-protectiveness might suggest her own unfortunate involvement with a 'bad' man.

Key point

Gladys regards Errol *'with awe'* (p.136), and as a purveyor of knowledge and wisdom. When Nan wants to know 'what it says in that there encyclops about the Aborigines' (p.135), Nan suspects there will be nothing.

Key vocabulary

Brylcreemed (p.132): slicked back with Brylcreem, a hair-styling product for men.

Came down with the last shower (p.135): is completely clueless.

Celestial (p.133): to do with the heavens; here the term (mockingly) suggests an aura of reverence generated by the encyclopedias.

Clapboard (p.134): 'clapboard' refers to timber board used on exterior house walls, or a device used in filmmaking and video production; the word in this context is likely an error for 'mortarboard': a square-topped black cap worn by students graduating from university.

Glowering (p.134): looking angry.

Kero (kerosene, p.133): a light fuel oil used in domestic heating.

Moom (p.137): Aboriginal term for 'bottom'.

She's the cat's mother (p.138): old-fashioned reproof to someone for calling a woman 'she' rather than using her name or title.

Snake-oil salesman (p.136): con man.

Q Is Nan right not to trust Errol at this point in the play? Explain your reasoning with reference to the text.

Q Gladys sings 'I've Got the World on a String' (p.136). Look up the words of the song and comment on their significance to the characters and/or events in the play. Also discuss the significance of other songs mentioned in the play.

Scene Three: Lino (pp.138–43)

Summary: *At the tip (and in a dream sequence) Dolly imagines that Daish's Paddock (the name of the tip) is a 'posh' store, and she is shopping there for 'linoleum' (lino floor covering, pp.138–9). Dolly walks home past the cork trees and Leon (who's drunk) asks her to join him and his mates.*

Errol suggests that Dolly moves to the city, where there is 'swags of work' (p.141), little realising the impossibility of her getting any job other than fruit picking in Mooroopna. His innocence of discriminatory attitudes implies his lack of prejudice, but also his naivety in thinking she could do 'anything' she wanted (p.141).

Key point

Returning from the tip, Dolly is questioned by Nan about whether she has gone near the cork trees. When she reassures her grandmother that those 'goomees' (Leon and his mates) are 'harmless', Nan reminds her that they are still 'our people' and deserve her 'respect' because 'they've had it hard' (p.139). Nan's steadfast loyalty to her people even extends to troublemakers.

Key vocabulary

Blue Moon (p.141): the local cannery.

Gina Lollobrigida (p.142): Italian actress and photojournalist in the 1960s who became an international sex symbol.

Goomees (p.139): drinkers (Aboriginal slang) – sometimes such terms are deliberately used to keep Indigenous languages alive.

Has a head of steam (p.142): description of someone who suddenly becomes very motivated.

Q Is politically correct language a necessity or a nuisance? Explain your reasoning with reference to the text.

Scene Four: House of Biba (pp.143–4)

Summary: *Papa Dear hasn't been home for three months because he's 'busy' doing 'good work' and 'God's work' (p.143); in Gladys' dream sequence he briefly enters the room. Dolly is hopeful of a summer job at Trevaks.*

With a job at Trevaks, Dolly thinks she might learn how to use the cash register and, more importantly, might also get offcuts that Nan could use to make clothes for the family. The ironic title of this scene humorously draws attention to the vast difference between up-market designer clothes and those made with remnants from a clothing-factory floor in Mooroopna. The irony is subtly embedded in the audience's expectation that garments from Biba would be vastly superior to anything Nan could make – especially with curtain material salvaged from the tip. Harrison cleverly subverts notions of British superiority, with Nan's dressmaking skills proving to be equal to those of a famous London designer. Moreover, with limited resources, Nan demonstrates considerable expertise and ingenuity. Harrison also draws attention to a 'cultural cringe' in the 1950s which deemed Australia culturally inferior, particularly in comparison with Britain and the United States. As a highly skilled Indigenous woman, Nan defies all expectations of antipodean inferiority.

Key point

Nan knows that a girl 'from The Flats' will not be considered for the job because 'her address' (p.144) will identify her as an Indigenous Australian. On the radio, Dolly Dyer praises the 'miracle' foaming action of Ajax, sounding (according to her husband, Bob), like an Ajax elf (p.144). In Nan's mind, elves and operating cash registers are part of an unattainable fantasy world.

Key vocabulary

Ajax (p.144): popular cleaning product containing bleach.

Q Are Papa Dear's long absences from his family justifiable? Explain your reasoning with reference to the text.

Scene Five: The Delivery (pp.144–50)

Summary: *Time has passed: Dolly and Errol look 'more mature' (p.144). Errol arrives with a parcel and Gladys is pleased, while Nan is openly hostile towards him. Outside, Errol asks Dolly if she'd like to go to a dance.*

Gladys is delighted with her new encyclopedia and tells Errol to call her 'Aunty' (p.146). Dolly agrees to go to the dance and arranges to meet Errol at the hall. The mood is broken abruptly when Nan suddenly appears and 'looks daggers' at Errol.

Key point

When Dolly reminds Errol that she is from The Flats, he replies that it is she who matters, not where she lives. Stage directions here seem to subtly map the trajectory of their future relationship: 'DOLLY *starts to move away but he grabs her*' and they dance *'perfectly together'* (p.149).

Key vocabulary

Aunty (p.146): with permission, an elder may be referred to as 'Aunty' in an Aboriginal community, as a sign of respect.

Jitterbug (p.149): a swing dance popular in America in the 1950s.

Mamel (p.145): a non-venomous carpet snake.

Scene Six: The Inspection (pp.150–4)

Summary: *The Inspector compliments Nan and Gladys on the whiteness of their white laundry. When he mentions assimilation, Nan worries that 'they' might take Dolly and 'make her work for someone', as they did with Gladys (p.154).*

Hurrying home from Ester's house, Dolly *'bursts in, as if she has something urgent to say'* (p.151). When the Inspector leaves, Dolly asks if she should go back to Ester's, but Nan suspects that it's 'probably too late now' (p.153) as the Inspector has probably already noticed signs of domestic violence and disarray.

Key point

The Inspector is astonished that 'the whites', washed in 'river water', are 'so white' (p.152), apparently assuming that the women's limited resources would make such effective washing unlikely. Gladys tersely dismisses the insult, declaring that she and Nan wash their sheets 'same as everyone' (p.152). There is a subtle racism in the idea of whiteness being so admirable and the suggestion that dark-skinned people might be unable to achieve it even in washing clothes.

Key vocabulary

Assimilation (p.154): an Australian government policy that was not abolished until 1973. The policy of assimilation was intended to integrate Aboriginal people into white society, but its associated policies of removing children from their families and denying them knowledge of their language and culture were extremely harmful.

Blue bag (p.152): a popular laundry product used to increase the whiteness of white fabrics.

Scene Seven: The Turn (pp.154–7)

Summary: *Gladys gets dressed to attend a fundraising meeting and Dolly dresses up to go out. When Nan realises that Dolly is not going with Gladys, she becomes extremely agitated – especially when she learns that Errol is taking Dolly to a dance.*

When Dolly appears, looking 'gorgeous' in a 'very tight-waisted 1950s dress', Nan suddenly realises that Dolly is no longer a 'baby' (p.155) and later Nan fakes a coughing fit to keep Dolly at home. Hearing Errol toot his horn outside, Nan's fake cough gets worse and, regretfully, Dolly cancels her plans and stays with Nan.

Key point

Listening to an advertisement on the radio for Ajax, Gladys comments on white people's obsession with 'whiteness' (p.155). This signals a significant change in Gladys, whose own obsession with whiteness was evident in Scene One (A) (pp.124–5).

Key vocabulary

Full up to pussy's bow (p.154): old-fashioned expression for having overeaten and feeling uncomfortably full.

Gubba (p.156): whitefella (in this case, Errol).

Rumbalara (p.155): Aboriginal housing estate near Mooroopna; the word means the end of the rainbow.

Scene Eight: Washing-Day Blues (pp.158–60)

Summary: *Ester's boys have not been at school and Dolly, suspecting they have been taken away, wonders whether that is why Ester is down at the cork trees, drinking alcohol.*

When she declares that she's now 'a woman' (p.158), Dolly reveals a wider perspective on her world. Like many adolescent girls, she measures herself against the dominant adolescent females around her, particularly white-skinned Nancy Woolthorpe and her friends. Dolly is torn between imitation of them and a need to be herself.

Key point

Images of cleanliness and whiteness pervade this scene. It is not coincidental that cleanliness and whiteness are so closely connected, nor that there are discriminatory racial connotations attached. The 'blue bags' whiten whites, but 'blues' also means sorrow and might symbolise First Nations Australians' abiding sadness over loss of Country.

Key vocabulary

Ernie Sigley (p.158): teen idol and popular actor, singer and radio presenter of the 1950s.

Peplum (p.160): a short gathered, frilled or pleated strip of fabric attached at the waist of a dress to create a hanging frill or flounce.

Scene Nine: Home Sweet Home (pp.160–2)

Summary: *Errol mentions the ball to Gladys, and reveals his hope of meeting Dolly there. After he leaves, Dolly and her mother exchange harsh and bitter words. When Nan arrives, family tensions escalate.*

The title of this scene is ironic as conflict erupts between the three (usually relatively close) family members. Offended by Dolly's confrontational manner, Gladys threatens her with physical punishment (with a wattle stick). Gladys' determination for Dolly to succeed sometimes clashes with Dolly's adolescent need for independence.

Key vocabulary

Different kettle of fish (p.162): expression meaning something is completely unlike a topic or situation previously discussed.

Home sweet home (p.160): an often-used expression of gladness when returning to a happy home. Used ironically, it indicates that the home is not happy.

Q Does Gladys encourage Dolly in a supportive way, or pressure her to succeed? Explain your reasoning with reference to the text.

Scene Ten: The Bank vs Mrs Banks (pp.163–5)

Summary: *Gladys visits the bank to discuss a traineeship for Dolly. Looking for reasons to refuse her request, the Bank Manager explains that she might not 'fit in' (because of her skin colour, p.163). Eventually, he helps Gladys fill in an application form, swayed perhaps by her plea to give Dolly the 'break' she 'deserves' (p.164).*

The Bank Manager offers Gladys a money box to put her 'pennies' in, and explains the importance of saving 'for something special' (p.164). Gladys suddenly hears Dolly's voice asking her if she has learned 'not to be shamed by them' (p.164). Ironically, the Bank Manager unintentionally shames Gladys by offering her a pen to fill in an application form, assuming she can read and write (p.165).

Key point

Dolly sings 'Catch a Falling Star' (a popular song in the 1950s) as she picks fruit in an orchard (p.163). In this context, the title of the song is ironic: catching a falling star (finding luck or happiness) seems to be an impossibility. This implies the unlikelihood of Dolly's being awarded a traineeship at the bank and suggests that she, like other local Aboriginal Australians, will probably become a fruit picker.

The song title also alludes to John Donne's sixteenth-century poem 'Go and catch a falling star' – a playful but misogynistic (prejudiced against women) poem about the inevitability of women's infidelity. Misogyny is also evident in the Bank Manager's condescension towards Gladys.

Key vocabulary

Gauze (p.163): thin, translucent fabric sometimes used as a screen. (This might also have metaphorical implications.)

Leaving Certificate (p.163): the certificate obtained at the end of school, equivalent to the VCE or HSC, although in the 1950s the final year of school was Year 11.

Pennies (p.164): imperial (British) currency, used in Australia until 1966. A penny was roughly the equivalent of one cent in Australian decimal currency.

Rapport (p.164): relationships or connections, usually involving respect, good communication and empathy.

Scene Eleven: The Ball (pp.165–7)

Summary: *Nancy is declared the winner of the Miss Mooroopna-Shepparton contest and announces that Dolly's dress is made from old curtains her parents had dumped at the tip. Humiliated, Dolly runs out. Hovering nearby is Leon, who roughly takes hold of her; when Errol steps in to protect her, Leon punches and injures him. Dolly, in tears, rushes away.*

Nancy and her friends critically scrutinise Dolly and Errol as they dance. Dolly looks 'much nicer' than Nancy (p.166), in Errol's opinion, and

Nancy needs to publicly assert her exaggerated sense of race and class superiority, while Leon, with his wounded male pride, decides to punish Dolly for thinking she's 'too good' for her own people (p.167).

Key point

Errol's transformation from stuttering salesman to suave romantic hero has an almost fairytale feel (p.165). He also becomes Dolly's gallant rescuer when she is physically accosted. The black eye he receives when Leon punches him (p.167) might be seen as a mark of his courage.

Key vocabulary

Big-band swing music (p.165): jazz style, especially popular in the 1950s.

Orchid corsage (p.165): small (expensive) floral arrangement worn on the bodice of a formal gown, often given by a young man to his girlfriend. Orchids are said to symbolise love.

Scene Twelve: Storm Brewing (pp.167–8)

Summary: *Gladys imagines Dolly enjoying herself at the ball, but Nan has a 'sense of foreboding' (p.168). She goes outside with the kero lamp and calls to Dolly; there is no reply and the wind extinguishes the light.*

Reference to a 'storm brewing' in the title of the scene suggests the likelihood of trouble. Nan's deep anxiety over Dolly seems to reflect something traumatic in Nan's own life, and it explains her obsessive need to protect her granddaughter. This is Harrison's reminder of how historical abuse remains palpably present in successive generations.

Key point

Details of phenomena in the natural world (such as those described in stage directions) are often symbolic of the characters' experiences in the play. Alone in a dark landscape, Dolly's isolation and vulnerability are accentuated by the sound of the 'rising wind' which also extinguishes Nan's lamp (p.168).

Scene Thirteen: Waters Rising (pp.168–72)

Summary: *Finding Dolly sobbing by the river, Errol comforts her, but they argue about whether she should move to the city with him. They part on unfriendly terms and Leon's menacing voice is heard offstage. His sinister words: 'Well, hello, Dolly' (p.172) refer (ironically) to a cheerful song from a Broadway musical.*

When asking Dolly about her family Christmas and 'pressies ... under the tree' (p.169) Errol prioritises his own cultural values and implicitly dismisses hers. Yet Dolly's hope for 'a tree and presents', and her wish to emulate Nancy Woolthorpe's family Christmases ('with all the trimmings', pp.169–70), reveal how the values and customs of powerful cultural majorities might eclipse those of marginalised cultures.

Key point

Dolly finds Errol's naive assumption that 'gin' was a reference to alcohol rather grimly amusing (p.170) as she is aware of the word's offensive sexual and racial connotations. Errol is also naive in trying to convince Dolly to move to the city, and in thinking that he is offering her 'the world'. Highly offended, she accuses him of discounting her world and, feeling *'utterly crushed'*, Errol walks away (p.172).

Key vocabulary

Aeroplane jelly (p.169): in the 1930s, Bert Appleroth (a tram conductor) created jelly crystals using gelatine and sugar in a bath. He used a Tiger Moth plane to deliver his product to rural areas and the jelly became a national icon.

Gin (p.170): (offensive) reference to an Indigenous Australian woman.

Gin jockey (p.170): a white man who has sexual relations with Indigenous Australian women.

Kelvinator (p.171): a brand of electrically powered refrigerator, which replaced the ice-chest in the early twentieth century.

Scene Fourteen: The Flood (pp.173–5)

Summary: *Nan and Gladys pack their belongings as the rain, thunder and lightning indicate another flood is imminent. A policeman (the Jungi) arrives to help them take 'the essentials' (p.173) to higher ground and Dolly arrives home, distraught.*

Horrified, Nan and Gladys realise what has happened to Dolly. The policeman tries to stop Dolly entering the humpy and, when she pushes past him, Gladys urges him to go and help another family (p.174). Left on the flooded ground, the encyclopedias are completely ruined.

Key point

The second verse of the song 'Que Sera, Sera', with its reference to fate as the determinant of human destiny, suggests that Dolly's fate is to follow in her grandmother's footsteps.

Key vocabulary

Banshee (p.175): (in Irish legend) a female spirit whose wailing warns of an imminent death.

ACT TWO

Scene One: After the Flood (pp.176–7)

Summary: *Nan, Gladys and Dolly survey the 'devastation'; Nan discovers the ruined encyclopedias (p.176). When Errol appears and apologises to Dolly, Gladys threatens him with an axe.*

Gladys is philosophical about the encyclopedias, which are 'only possessions' while people are 'what matters' (p.176); this reinforces the importance of family and community.

Errol's apology is for leaving Dolly alone and defenceless in the dark, not – as it seems to Nan and Gladys – for sexually assaulting her. Errol leaves, utterly devastated by their belief that he would rape Dolly.

Key point

Dolly's revelation that her attacker 'wasn't him' shocks Nan and Gladys, who were quick to blame Errol (p.177). The sound of bulldozers in the background demolishing the ruined buildings symbolises the apparent disintegration of Errol and Dolly's relationship.

Key vocabulary

Shell-shocked (p.176): a term initially used to describe soldiers traumatised by war.

Scene Two: The Move to Rumbalara (pp.177–8)

Summary: *A radio broadcast announces the proposed relocation of flood victims to 'neat, new, prefabricated' houses (p.178).*

The new houses are *'small, white and featureless'*. Nan becomes grimly positive and talks of making curtains (p.178), again showing her resilience and ability to make a fresh start after a crisis.

Key point

By comparison with the substandard housing at Rumbalara, the economic reforms instigated by US President Franklin Roosevelt in 1933 – referred to as the 'New Deal' – provided jobs and financial relief to many needy American people. In Australia, there was also a 'New Deal' policy, announced in 1939 by the federal Minister for the Interior John McEwan and closely aligned with the policy of assimilation (Australian Human Rights Commission 2010). Nan's use of the phrase (p.178) is bitterly ironic.

Scene Three: The Broadcast (pp.178–82)

Summary: *Dolly receives a letter from the bank but refuses to open it. She and Gladys argue. Frustrated by Gladys' constant pressure on her, Dolly challenges her mother to 'fix' her own 'house' – that is, deal with her own issues (p.179). The radio announcer is broadcasting live from the local Shire Council meeting (p.180).*

Dolly seems to have given up any hope of a career, and her deep disappointment is directed at her mother. Listening to Dolly's angry words, something 'snaps' in Gladys, who walks out (p.179). On the radio is the broadcast of the council meeting and Gladys' voice is heard interrupting the proceedings. She has risen to the challenge to 'fix up' her 'own house' by championing the rights of her people (p.179).

Key point

Gladys reminds the councillors that her people didn't 'choose' to live on a flood plain, and are not 'welcome' in the town (p.181). As she is ejected, Gladys' final, and strongest, point is her defiant assertion that the land belongs to her.

Key vocabulary

Ablutions (p.180): washing and toilet facilities.

Bee in her bonnet (p.179): a persistent or obsessive belief or idea that someone cannot get out of their head.

Flabbergasted (p.182): very surprised.

Night cart (p.180): before modern sanitary plumbing, chamber pots (potties) and unplumbed outside toilets were used. The contents of these were collected each night by men in horse-drawn carts.

Piccaninny (p.180): a small, black-skinned child (now considered a racist term).

Schizenhausen (p.182): very low quality (colloquial translation/usage: 'shithouse').

Q Why might Dolly refuse to open the letter from the bank? Explain your reasoning with reference to the text.

Scene Four: The Contract (pp.182–4)

Summary: *Errol arrives to see Gladys about the contract she signed to pay off the encyclopedias. Gladys apologises for her former hostility towards him, and he helps her write an application for a cancellation of the contract.*

Errol asks about Dolly, hoping to see her, but Gladys says Dolly has 'changed' and won't want to see him; Errol insists that *he* will change and will become 'worthy' of her (p.184). This is a promising sign, considering Errol's previous expectation, that Dolly would happily become part of his supposedly superior world in the city.

Key point

At the end of the scene, the song 'Catch a Falling Star', with its directive to do the impossible, suggests the strength of Errol's determination to win Dolly back. Gladys takes on a challenge as well – summoning the courage to learn to read and write (p.184).

Key vocabulary

Shillings … into the meter box (p.182): coins fed into the electricity meter to enable power supply.

Q Male characters in the play (apart from Errol) are unsympathetically portrayed. What makes Errol different?

Scene Five: Pay the Rent (pp.184–8)

Summary: *The Rent Collector decides that an 'impending new arrival' in the house will make the accommodation unsuitable (p.185). When he reprimands Nan for 'flouting … the rules' in relation to the midwife's visit she tells him to 'go to blazes' and pelts him with eggs (pp.185–6).*

Nan tells Dolly that she and Errol cannot marry (despite their love for each other) because a young white man, whose name was Clem Fisher, 'took advantage' of her when she was seventeen (p.187): a secret she doesn't want Gladys to know. (Errol is also a Fisher, so Nan worries that he and Dolly could be related.) The secrets between Nan and Dolly (p.188) strengthen their bonds of love and trust.

Key point

The song 'Somewhere Over the Rainbow', which plays at the beginning of this scene, alludes to *The Wizard of Oz*, with its reminder of Dorothy's yearning to return home. This is also a sharp reminder that First Nations Australians have had their land taken from them, that their new homes are unsuitable and that happy endings usually only happen in Hollywood movies.

Key vocabulary

Disdain (p.185): contempt, disapproval.

Finito (p.188): (Italian) finished.

Go to blazes (p.186): go to hell.

Knight in shining armour (p.187): heroic rescuer of helpless young women.

Layette (p.188): a collection of baby clothing and nursery items.

Scene Six: Errol Spills the Beans (pp.189–91)

Summary: *Errol offers Gladys a 'bonus volume' of the encyclopedia but it no longer interests her (p.189). They discuss Dolly, and there are promising signs that their relationship might be mended.*

Gladys makes a sheepish reference to her 'radio moment' and reveals that her own people are 'cranky' with her for 'drawing attention' to them (p.189). By contrast, Papa Dear's public appearances gain him widespread approval and an audience with the Queen (p.128).

Errol tells Gladys that what he likes about Dolly is that she is 'very pretty' and Gladys needs to prompt him about Dolly's other attributes: she is also 'clever', 'kind', 'modest' and 'straightforward' (p.190). When Errol wonders how straightforward Dolly is with him, Gladys encourages him to talk to Dolly (p.191).

Key vocabulary

Snotty googles (p.191): Errol's mispronunciation of 'snooty goggles' (p.147), i.e. wattle gum.

Spills the beans (p.189): reveals confidential or private information.

Scene Seven: The Petition (pp.191–9)

Summary: *Looking at Dolly's baby, Errol realises what happened to Dolly on the night of the ball; he apologises and offers to help her. Errol and Nan's relationship is mended by his kindness to her when she becomes ill at the meeting, and she advises Dolly to marry him once she realises he is not related to Gladys' biological father. Papa Dear does not arrive in time to speak at the meeting, so Gladys steps up.*

Errol offers to move to Shepparton because of Dolly's family's importance to her. Dolly initially refuses his offer, yet Nan's dream sequence with wedding bells and confetti, and her advice to Dolly to marry him 'before someone else does' (p.198), provide a traditional romantic ending and (with Dolly's nursing scholarship, p.191) the promise of a brighter future.

Key point

As the play ends, the words of the song 'Que Sera, Sera' suggest that what 'will be' is *not* predetermined when people are empowered to take control of their circumstances.

Key vocabulary

Bex (p.194): pain-relieving medicinal powder.

Lepers (p.198): carriers of an infectious disease affecting the skin and nervous system.

Mrs Windsor (p.197): somewhat disrespectful reference to Queen Elizabeth II.

'The Old Rugged Cross' (p.194): sentimental American Christian song.

To boot (p.197): as well.

CHARACTERS & RELATIONSHIPS

Dolly

Key quote

'And as far as what you're offering ... no thank you. This is my place. I'm staying right here with my mum and my nan.' (to Errol, p.172)

As the play opens, Dolly surveys the flood damage. Noticing her ruined magazines, she decides to say nothing, indicating a practised stoicism in the face of misfortune. Dolly is also studious, completing her Leaving Certificate with all 'As and Bs' and coming 'top of her class in algebra' (p.163). She is remarkably 'pretty' (p.190) but (as Gladys reminds Errol) she is also 'clever', kind', 'modest' and 'straightforward'. Dolly sometimes allows herself to dream; she imagines Gladys winning luxurious prizes on *Pick-A-Box* (p.130), and dreams of winning the Miss Mooroopna-Shepparton title at the ball (p.166). Rather fancifully she (like many teenage girls) would like to be an actress or a model, but on a more practical level she dreams of a career as a nurse (p.142). She is, however, unhappily aware that she might become a fruit picker, like her mother and grandmother (p.141). Dolly's exposure to racial discrimination, with 'stones' thrown at her, and 'snide remarks' (p.162) overheard in the street, make her pessimistic about her future.

Dolly has a close and loving relationship with Nan, whose over-protectiveness can occasionally become tedious. Yet their closeness and trust alleviate Dolly's distress when, after she becomes pregnant, Nan confides in her that Gladys was conceived in similarly traumatic circumstances. The sharing of this dark 'secret' brings them both great comfort.

Nan

Key quote

'Ask him what it says in that there encyclops about the Aborigines, eh?' (to Gladys, p.135)

Nan is often the cynical voice of experience muttering in the background, reminding Gladys that she is a lowly bean picker who is unworthy of the Queen's notice (p.124). Unafraid to speak out where her family is concerned, Nan's anger is aroused by the Rent Collector's criticism of their 'flouting' of the 'rules' regarding the midwife's visit; she declares that she doesn't care about his rules and throws eggs at him (pp.185–6). She is a capable, energetic woman, working as a fruit picker for the canning factory. She tackles the hard physical work of cooking, cleaning and washing, and can make a stew out of nettles (stinging plants) when money for food is short. Also a skilled dressmaker, Nan transforms discarded curtains from the tip into a 'gorgeous' ball gown for Dolly (p.160).

Nan is a loving and protective grandmother to Dolly and knows, from her own bitter experience, the danger of being '[taken] advantage of' by 'a whitefella' (p.187). Like some older people, Nan is set in her ways; she sees Bob Dyer as 'one of them flash Yanks' (p.131) and is wary of Errol, initially regarding him as a 'snake-oil salesman' (p.136). She is also doubtful about the masculinity of a man who 'smells of perfume' (p.136) and whose 'hands are too soft' (p.195). Eventually, she recognises the goodness in Errol and advises Dolly to marry him 'before someone else does' (p.198).

While Nan is supportive of Gladys, like most mothers and daughters they have their disagreements. Nan criticises Gladys' monarchist sympathies (p.124) and is dubious about the importance of Dolly's education. Nan and Gladys also clash over what Gladys sees as Nan's disregard for her maternal authority over Dolly when Nan tells Dolly she can attend the ball (p.162). After hearing the radio broadcast of Gladys' disruption at the first council meeting, Nan's immense pride in her daughter is expressed in the 'little jig' she and Dolly dance around the radio, and Nan admits: 'I didn't think you had it in you, daught' (p.182). The strength of Nan's commitment to family is also, rather touchingly, displayed in her insistence on setting a place at the dinner table for Papa Dear, who hasn't been home for 'three months' (p.143).

Gladys

Key quote

'"We demand proper schooling." [*To herself*] And not just for us. [*Continuing*] "The white people too – they need to be educated about us, and our ways."' (p.197)

Initially a fervent royalist, Gladys goes to extraordinary lengths to get a 'squiz' (p.124) at the Queen during the royal tour. Her attempt is thwarted by the hessian screens lining the streets and hiding Indigenous Australians' unsightly humpies from the royal gaze (p.127). Gladys is also clever; she is able to correctly answer all the questions on the radio quiz show *Pick-A-Box,* but won't take up Dolly's suggestion to become a contestant, suspecting that a 'black' contestant (even one who would not be seen) would be unwelcome (pp.129–30). On the practical side, she can chop wood and skin rabbits (p.129), and is a competent financial manager, with coins stored in jam tins allocated to various household expenses. This makes the Bank Manager's white male condescension (p.164) particularly ludicrous. Having been 'sent off to work for a family' as a child (p.184) and never having had the opportunity to complete her education, Gladys is embarrassed by her inability to read and write, and determined that her clever daughter will achieve what she could not. Gladys often slips into reveries, in which dreams seem to become reality: from being hugged by the Queen (p.126) to seeing Dolly as a graduate in an academic cap and gown (p.134). These comforting 'daydreams' nurture a hope that they will, one day, '*come true*' (p.154).

Gladys and Dolly sometimes clash; Dolly feels pressured by her mother's ambitious plans for her, and she tells her mother to 'fix' her own house (p.179). Gladys does this by becoming a vocal political activist. Redirecting her energy towards improving the lives of her people, she barges into a council meeting, disrupting it with her loud objections to the councillors' inappropriate proposals for solving the 'so-called housing problem' (p.181). She also takes on the challenge of learning to read, and delivers an articulate and passionate speech at a later, more significant meeting. Through her remarkable political transformation, and in a gutsy display of feminist agency, Gladys speaks for Papa Dear and becomes the nationalistic voice of her people (pp.196–8). In this way, Gladys conveys Harrison's message that a courageous and committed individual can be a vital part of a push for political change.

Errol

Key quote

'This is my first presentation. Well, the first one I got all the way through, anyhow.' (p.137)

Scene Two (A) is titled 'Oh, Errol' although Errol does not appear until Scene Two (B). The title is likely an allusion to a song by the popular 1980s rock band Australian Crawl about the handsome and suave Australian actor Errol Flynn, who became a Hollywood star in the 1950s. The title of the scene is meant to be ironic, as Harrison's character is awkward and incompetent. Having become lost and confused, Errol takes a wrong turn and ends up at The Flats instead of the part of town 'where all the toffs live' (p.135). His presentation is comically inept and he needs help from Gladys to get through it. In a play with so many unsympathetically constructed male characters, it is Errol's difference from them that makes him so acceptable.

Errol's ignorance and naivety are evident in his fear of a (non-venomous) carpet snake (p.145) and in his innocent interpretation of 'gin jockey' (p.170); yet, curiously, these characteristics add to his appeal. The narrative thread following the relationship between Errol and Dolly unfolds in the manner of popular romance fiction, structured around the ups and downs of their relationship. The high point is the ball, where Errol transforms himself into a charming and gallant hero, complimenting Dolly on her appearance and rescuing her from the villain, Leon (p.167). Humorously, a comparison with Errol Flynn might not be unimaginable here.

The low point comes after the ball when Errol offends Dolly by suggesting she forsake her home and family and move, with him, to an allegedly 'better life' in the city (p.171). She refuses his offer to walk her home and, 'utterly crushed' (p.172), Errol walks away. Believing it is Errol who has raped Dolly, Gladys and Nan become hostile and he is no longer welcome in their home. Errol is determined to win Dolly back, and makes a commitment to move to Mooroopna to be with her. His comment to Gladys about liking 'snotty googles' (using Indigenous Australian vernacular, p.191, though perhaps a mispronunciation of Dolly's early 'snooty goggles', p.147), suggests that he might be able to fully embrace an Indigenous Australian culture.

Leon

Key quote

'She's no lady, she's just a little –' (to Errol, referring to Dolly, p.167)

Leon hangs around with the cork-tree lads who tend to view young women merely as sex objects. The offensive word left unspoken by Leon implies Dolly's promiscuity and, in his mind, justifies his attempted and actual sexual assaults on her. While his behaviour is inexcusable, Nan's reference to the boys having 'had it hard' (p.139) alludes to a wider issue: the education of Indigenous Australians – particularly young men – has often been inadequate or unsuited to their needs, thus employment opportunities are limited and alcoholism is rife. Added to this is Nan's muted comment about Leon being a 'motherless child' (p.131). The government at the time did nothing to address these issues.

Papa Dear

Key quote

> '... that's how important [the Queen] is – getting a meeting with the busiest Aboriginal around!' (Nan, referring to Papa Dear, p.128)

Papa Dear is conspicuous by his absence throughout the play, while the women in his family deal with devastating floods and challenging family issues. The women work hard, sometimes doing extra shifts at the canning factory (p.140) to put food on the table. As a pastor who does 'good work' (p.143), Papa Dear has made a name for himself: one which even the Inspector recognises. Papa Dear has clearly embraced Christianity as a way of having a voice that is respected by white Australians, yet it seems that he has done very little to make life better for First Nations Australians. Despite this, he is granted a meeting with the Queen, although this might seem like tokenism from a government that hid Aboriginal Australians' humpies from view to avoid embarrassing the British monarch (p.127). Like many powerful and successful men, Papa Dear has furthered his career by spending most of his time away from his family – it is the women who hold this family together.

The Inspector

Key quote

> 'Speak to your local MPs. Form a delegation. Collect petitions. Write letters. Inform yourself. Knowledge is power, ladies.' (p.152)

The Inspector is one of several self-important government officials who enjoy their power over vulnerable people. He boasts that 'things will change' as a result of his report (p.152), but this refers (rather ominously) to the Assimilation Policy. He also insists that the women must 'rally' themselves and 'take leadership' (p.152), but his advice shows no understanding of Indigenous Australians' circumstances, or of whether they have the resources to follow his recommendations. His ludicrous proposal aims to shift responsibility for political and social change onto people who may not be adequately educated and are perhaps even struggling to manage a household – as Ester is (p.131). His assurance that he 'will do all [he] can' (p.152) suggests that nothing will change.

The Rent Collector (Mr Coody)

Key quote

'Your arrangements will need to be re-evaluated, with the impending new arrival.' (to Nan, referring to Dolly's pregnancy, p.185)

The Rent Collector's disapproving male gaze assesses Dolly as an immoral and irresponsible young woman. When he insists that the family's arrangements will need to be 're-evaluated' (p.185), Nan's response – that their home is not Mr Coody's 'concern' – is an implicit criticism of the government's total *lack* of concern for adequate Aboriginal housing in the first place (p.185). His haughty assertion that it *is* his concern is an attempt to impose his bureaucratic authority. So, too, is his questioning of Nan about the person he saw leaving the house. When he reprimands Nan for 'flouting ... the rules' regarding the midwife's home visit, she tells him to 'go to blazes' (p.186) and throws eggs at him, showing her frustration not just with the Rent Collector but also with the bureaucracy he represents.

The Bank Manager

Key quote

'Now, rapport with our customers is important – sorry, rapport means ...' (to Gladys, p.164)

In the 1950s, a bank manager was an important person and, in a regional area like Mooroopna, he would be in the top rank of the social hierarchy. Harrison's Bank Manager is brimming with self-importance. Despite having two cups and saucers on his desk, he makes himself a cup of tea but doesn't offer Gladys one, aiming to demonstrate both his own elevated status and her lowly one (p.163). This is not only bad-mannered but also racist and misogynistic in its assumption that it is unnecessary to provide basic hospitality to an Aboriginal Australian woman. His supposition that financial mismanagement has perhaps landed Gladys in debt, and that she has come to ask about a loan (p.163), is also demeaning in its assumption that women and First Nations people are incompetent in dealing with money matters.

When Gladys mentions the possibility of a teller's traineeship for Dolly (p.163), the Bank Manager is caught off guard and scrambles for excuses to refuse her request. He wonders whether Dolly would 'fit in' (because of her skin colour) and questions her 'reliability' (endorsing stereotyped views about First Nations people's alleged unreliability). Also racist and sexist is his patronising attempt to explain the meaning of rapport (p.164). When Gladys interrupts him with a precise definition of the word, she angrily challenges his assumption. Ironically, the Bank Manager shows a complete lack of rapport in his dealings with Gladys, and his discriminatory views are representative of an Anglocentric, male-dominated social hierarchy in mid-twentieth-century Australia.

Nancy Woolthorpe

Key quote

'Love your dress, Dolly. Love the fabric. [*With a giggle*] My mother quite liked it too. When it was our sunroom curtains. But, you know, I thought we took them to the tip.' (p.166)

Nancy is the stereotypical 'mean girl': well-to-do and pretty, and she is surrounded by gutless admirers who would rather be dominated by her than victimised by her. Dolly is impressed by Nancy's family's Christmas, with its artificial tree and all the 'trimmings' (pp.169–70), and Nancy's mother (like Errol's) is 'at home' and has nothing to do but 'bake and dust' (p.170). Errol tells Dolly that her family has 'more fun' than his family, and by implication, more than Nancy's family; what might be missing from Nancy's and Errol's families is the love that binds Dolly's family together.

The Jungi (policeman)

Key quote

'You can't go in there. We're evacuating.' (to Dolly, p.174)

The policeman shows little sympathy for the women whose house and possessions have been destroyed by the flood, or perhaps he is daunted by the scale of the disaster he is assigned to deal with. He is unresponsive to Dolly's distress and becomes angry when she disobeys his order not to enter the house. When Gladys explains the importance of the encyclopedias, he reassures her that they will be put somewhere 'high and dry' (p.174) but when he leaves, at Gladys' request, to help another family, he puts the crate of encyclopedias on the flooded ground and walks away. Yet the Jungi is apparently the only policeman helping the flood victims and is ill-equipped to respond to the family's emotional distress. The lack of appropriate support, for both the flood victims and the solitary policeman, indicates their lack of importance to those who are responsible for their wellbeing.

The Shire Councillors

Key quote

'Order! I must insist ... The Chair does not recognise this ... There are protocols! If you read the rules –' (Council Chairman to Gladys, p.181)

The voice of Councillor 1 is heard on the radio, complaining that the 'shanties' the Council had bulldozed on 'Crown Land' (Daish's Paddock) are 'creeping back', and warning that a 'lack of sanitation poses a serious risk' to the townspeople (p.180). Gladys, however, insists that the real issue is that The Flats are on a flood plain, while Daish's Paddock is on higher ground, and the Council plans to build sanitation facilities for the town instead of safer housing. When Councillor 1 refers to Daish's Paddock as something that 'serves the whole of our community, not just an itinerant minority' (p.181), he ignores the fact that Indigenous families living on The Flats are not itinerants and that they 'are not welcome in the townships' (p.181). Gladys also reminds him that their homes are often completely inundated. When the orderliness of the meeting disintegrates, the Chairman demands the ejection of the 'interloper' (p.181), and as she is led out Gladys pointedly reminds the councillors that this is her land.

Ester and her boys

A young Indigenous woman, Ester, the mother of three unruly boys, is pregnant again and her 'whitefella husband' (p.132) has given her a black eye. When the Inspector visits Ester's home, Nan fears that Ester's boys will be taken away (p.153). Indeed, this appears to be exactly what has happened when Dolly tells Nan that the boys have not been at school and that Ester is 'down at the cork trees' drinking with the men (p.158). The consequences of her boys being taken are catastrophic for Ester and (probably) for her unborn child. The reality, for Ester's boys, is that their 'assimilation' will involve adoption or institutionalisation, as well as separation from their family and community, and probably from each other. Removing vulnerable children from their families, their communities and their culture will exacerbate rather than resolve their problems.

THEMES, IDEAS & VALUES

The importance of home

Key quote

'They forced us to leave. Forced us to leave Cummeragunja. Our home.' (Nan, p.126)

The ramshackle humpy on The Flats, with its dirt floors and hessian walls, mostly provides the comfort and security the Dear family needs, but it is the close-knit family members who make it a home. Dolly tells Errol that 'a real home is where there are people looking out for each other', and insists that she wouldn't trade places with Nancy 'for anything' (p.172). The Rent Collector finds the Dears' accommodation unsuitable given the 'impending arrival' (p.185) of Dolly's child, yet it has always been substandard, with or without a baby coming. As the person responsible for 'Aboriginal Housing' (p.185), the Rent Collector has obviously failed to do his job. So, too, has the Shire Council, which has neither fixed the problems on The Flats nor resolved the larger problem of inadequate Aboriginal housing (p.181). Clearly, the irresponsible attitude of the government extends to all administrative matters connected with First Nations peoples' welfare.

By contrast, modern suburban homes in the 1950s had 'everything that opens and shuts' (p.172), reflecting the values of a white consumer-driven middle-class culture. Nancy's family has a 'great big fake' Christmas tree, and a mother whose main role is to 'bake and dust' (pp.169–70). Errol's view of a 'real home' is a 'sweet little flat with a balcony and a sitting room and a kitchen with a real stove and a new-fangled Kelvinator' (p.171). Errol's and Dolly's diametrically opposed views of 'home' contribute to the temporary breakdown of their relationship.

Nan's bitterness at being forced out of her home at Cummeragunja Station, on the banks of the Murray River (p.126), and her wish to return there to die (p.125), suggests a deeply embedded sense of belonging to a particular place and a strong connection with people who have lived there. The physical landscape itself becomes suffused with the notion of home: with the comfort and security that a home can offer.

Key point

Indigenous Australian people's relationship with the land is geosophical (earth-centred) in their belief that the land is 'impregnated with the power of the Ancestor Spirits' (Australians Together 2017). A key feature of Aboriginal spirituality is caring for the land, an obligation that has been passed down as law for thousands of years. Harrison reinforces her point about the importance of home by drawing on the imagery of popular culture. The belief that 'there's no place like home' is subtly affirmed by Harrison's allusion to *The Wizard of Oz* (p.184); this is a reminder that a place to call home is necessary to people's wellbeing.

The importance of family

Key quote

'No matter how [babies] come into the world, you still love 'em the same.'
(Nan to Dolly, p.186)

Immediate family

In *Rainbow's End*, the loving and mutually supportive biological relationships in the Dear family include 'three blood brothers' (p.169) who are permanently 'off working' (p.151). Within the cramped and makeshift domestic space of the humpy, however, family relationships are tested. Dolly and Gladys, for example, sometimes clash as a consequence of Gladys' strong hope that Dolly will achieve the success that she herself could not. Despite such moments, the family is bound together by the struggle to cope with poverty, injustice and devastating floods. In their determination to survive, these strong, independent women embody the ideals of family life: they nurture and protect each other and respect the humanitarian values that underpin a fair and safe society.

Dolly's question about their family tree (p.124) raises awkward and painful issues for Nan, likely relating to the secret Nan later shares with Dolly, about being '[taken] advantage of' by 'a whitefella' who went off to fight in the Great War (pp.186–7). Nan's reassurance that Dolly will love her baby, despite the dreadful circumstances of its conception, gives Dolly confidence that she, too, can overcome her traumatic ordeal. Nan's sharing of her past with Dolly places both their stories within a wider context of the vulnerability of women (and particularly First Nations women) in patriarchal societies. The sharing and passing down of family stories builds strong connections across the generations.

Extended family and community

Dolly's extended family includes aunts and uncles, and 'twenty-seven boy cousins' (p.169). As well as this kinship connection, many Indigenous Australians in the wider community are connected by their involvement in the quest for social justice. This is indicated by the approving words 'hear, hear' from the crowd offstage when Gladys refuses to 'humbly' beg and instead demands 'suitable housing for the Aboriginal people' (p.196). Dolly's immediate family is already well-known in the wider community through Papa Dear's 'good work' (p.143), and his meeting with the Queen (p.128) makes him a symbol of hope for his oppressed people. Likewise, Gladys' inspirational 'petition' speech (pp.196–8) is a pivotal moment, where a 'humble' plea is replaced by an explicit demand for social justice (p.197). The '*tumultuous applause*' (p.198) that follows her speech suggests that she has become a voice for Indigenous people as they unite behind her in a quest for equality. A further source of inspiration is Dolly's nursing scholarship (p.191), making her a potential role model for future generations of her people.

Key point

The Dears' strong connection to the local community provides a contrast with the narrow focus on individual and immediate family in western cultures (like Errol's and Nancy's families.) Nan's gift of a skinned rabbit (p.131) shows neighbourly concern for Ester, who has a black eye, and another child on the way (pp.131–2). Dolly, too, worries about Ester, who apparently seeks solace in sex and alcohol with the cork-tree lads when her boys are taken (p.158). After the catastrophic second flood, Gladys' request that the Jungi leave her precious encyclopedias and help a family with six children (p.174) celebrates the altruism embedded in a strong community spirit.

Identity

Key quote

'I'm from The Flats. Not even one of those townie types of cross-over Aboriginals.' (Dolly to Errol, p.149)

Both Gladys and Dolly sometimes seem to be caught between two cultures. Gladys' need for white gloves to greet the Queen, and her willingness to walk almost six kilometres in uncomfortable white high heels (p.127), show her emulating the 1950s dress codes for white, middle-class women. Nan is highly critical of Gladys' devotion to the Queen (p.124) and her loyalty to the British monarchy. Dolly, too, is critical of her mother for urging her to compete with Nancy for the traineeship at the bank (p.158), feeling that Gladys wants her to pretend 'to be one of them [white girls]' (p.158).

Yet Dolly herself is willing to compete with the white girls. Not only does she participate in their rituals by attending the Miss Mooroopna-Shepparton Ball, but she also dreams of winning the title (p.166). The ball becomes a key moment in Harrison's focus on the motif of identity as Dolly journeys towards a stronger affirmation of her Indigenous Australian heritage, particularly when she talks with Errol after they leave the hall and she asserts, 'This is my place' (p.172). Gladys, too, resolutely embraces her culture when she fights for her people's rights, turning away from her earlier loyalty to the monarchy.

Key point

Dolly's use of Aboriginal vernacular and her *'loud blackfella accent'* when she threatens to kick Ester's boys 'up the moom' (p.137), along with her reference to 'goomees' (p.139), can be seen as part of a resurgent First Nations cultural identity. This was almost obliterated during the years of assimilation, when the speaking of Indigenous languages was banned in order to absorb the 'Aborigine' into 'the [white] community' (p.152).

Harrison's play also suggests that the colonialist land-grab mentality was still flourishing in the 1950s, when the banishing of First Nations Australians to flood plains confirmed their status as social outcasts.

Gender and patriarchy

Key quote

'Listen, fella. Do you have any idea what'll happen if you walk into that dance with me?' (Dolly to Errol, p.148)

Masculinity

In western and westernised societies, stereotyped notions of masculinity include assertiveness and aggression as signs of manliness (although, taken to extremes, masculinity becomes 'toxic', as Leon's does). It is also expected that men are courageous, like Errol, who protects Dolly from Leon's unwelcome advances (p.167). In their personal relationships, too, these expectations insist that men should be firmly in control, as Errol's conservative father is, in his insistence that Errol should call him 'sir', and in his disapproval of his wife's 'funny' ideas about getting a job (p.170). Yet while most men internalise the need to avoid displays of soft-heartedness or vulnerability, what makes Errol an appealing character is the way he reveals this vulnerability when he stumbles his way through his presentation (p.133) and confesses to his anxiety. With his 'lousy sense of direction' (p.168), Errol often struggles to find his way, not only geographically but also metaphorically, in a world where the notions of traditional masculinity he has been brought up with don't always accommodate the independent ways of women like Dolly, who can look after herself (p.170) and who, along with her strong-minded family, values her 'own' way of life – imperfect as it might seem to Errol (p.172).

In Harrison's play, institutional and social power is held solely by male characters. The power of Papa Dear, as pastor and spokesperson for his people, makes him worthy of an audience with the Queen (p.128), even though his 'good works' (p.150) have not significantly improved the lives of his people. Other male authority figures use their positions solely for self-aggrandisement. Government officials spout bureaucratic jargon, endorsing 'assimilation' (p.152) and using veiled threats about 'rules' (p.185) to compensate themselves for their lack of any real power; Nan's egg-throwing pointedly reminds the Rent Collector of this lack of power (p.186). Male dominance is also subtly portrayed in the radio broadcasts of Bob Dyer's *Pick-A-Box*, a program in which the male quiz-master is superior in knowledge and intellect, while his wife's role is to praise the sponsor's domestic cleaning products. Dyer's patronising comment that his wife 'sounds like one of the elves in the commercial' (p.144) further trivialises her.

Toxic masculinity

The term 'toxic masculinity' refers to particular cultural norms associated with harm done to society by violent men, which often also damages the men themselves. Their misogynistic view categorises women as mere objects whose only purpose is to satisfy men's demands. Behaviour is considered 'toxic' when it includes sexual assault and domestic violence. Ester's 'whitefella' husband's actions, for example, harm not only his pregnant wife (p.129) but also his sons, who are taken into protective custody (p.158). Leon Arnold also exemplifies toxic masculinity. He is a menacing presence as he watches, stalks (p.139, p.169) and, eventually, rapes Dolly (p.172). As one of the alcoholic cork-tree lads, his behaviour harms both himself and those around him.

Stereotypical femininity

Femininity describes a set of attributes, behaviours and roles imposed on women and girls and normalised by patriarchal society. Traditionally, society's top tier has consisted of white, heterosexual men of high social standing, along with the monarch of the day, whether male or female. On the lowest tier were races other than white, the lower classes and (apart from royalty) females. In Harrison's play, the characters who display the most unpleasant versions of stereotyped femininity are Nancy Woolthorpe and her sycophantic friends. The girls are bitchy and competitive – perhaps succumbing to jealousy and judging Dolly on the basis of her (allegedly inferior) attire and her low social standing (p.166).

Women such as Nancy's and Errol's mothers are defined solely in terms of traditional domestic roles such as baking and dusting, although Errol's mother has 'funny ideas' (according to Errol's conservative father) about wanting to 'get a job' (p.170). Nan and Gladys take on domestic roles (cooking and washing) as well, but they also work shifts at the Blue Moon cannery (p.140). Yet Gladys knows how to wield an axe to chop wood (p.129, p.182); Nan can kill and skin a rabbit for dinner (p.129) and, like Cinderella's fairy godmother, can transform cast-off fabric into a beautiful ball gown (p.166). These independent and competent female characters have none of the traits deemed necessary for women in a conservative patriarchal society. These include modesty, docility, subservience and humility, and are meant to keep women in their place and prevent any challenge to male power.

Errol, too, has conservative ideas about women. By referring to Dolly as 'a lady' (p.167), Errol interrupts Leon's crude insult, but by doing so he, too, stereotypes her. This label defines a woman who complies with patriarchal expectations regarding 'ladylike' behaviour (like Errol's mother's female submissiveness). Moreover, a 'lady' must not display intellectual superiority over men; with this in mind, Nan warns Gladys of the danger of getting 'knocked down' if she gets 'too clever' (p.155). Dolly Dyer (at least in her radio persona) is the typically vacuous and pretty celebrity wife (p.144). A married 'lady' is apparently happy to be domesticated, like Mrs Woolthorpe: the perfect housewife who is content to 'bake and dust' day after day (p.170). These socially acceptable female role models were celebrated in 1950s American television shows designed to lure women (who had taken men's jobs during World War II) back into the home where they allegedly belonged. After the arrival of second-wave feminism in the early 1960s, the word 'lady' carried negative connotations regarding such compliant behaviour. Dolly Banks is an assertive and clever young woman who plans to be a working mother and is clearly not a 'lady'.

The male gaze

The phrase 'male gaze' describes the (not always literal or physical) scrutinising of young women in ways that empower men, while sexualising and objectifying the women. Although young men and women sometimes assess each other as potential partners, which might describe the *'instant spark of attraction'* that passes between Dolly and Errol (p.132), the 'male gaze' is disempowering and reductive. It is a means by which heterosexual males (or patriarchal society in general) tend to scrutinise, dominate and exploit women for their own purposes. Leon is the obvious exemplar of this with his assessment of Dolly as a 'party girl' and his invitation for her to 'join' him and his mates (p.139).

Looking at a photo of Dolly, the Bank Manager observes that she has a 'very pretty face' (p.163). While not assessing her as a potential sexual conquest, his narrow focus on her appearance is characteristic of the male gaze. This, indeed, is the case with beauty contests where young women compete for male attention; these competitions shape male and female perceptions of women's worth, their roles, their sexuality and their power. Leon's male gaze is highly predatory. At the ball, he waits until Dolly is alone and tries to force himself on her. Interrupted by Errol, he begins to insult her with a highly offensive term, and justifies his intentions by alleging that Dolly is the kind of loose woman who encourages men's advances (p.167). When he later rapes her (p.172), he satisfies his need to teach her 'a lesson' (p.167): one which is also about the perceived impropriety of mixed-race relationships. Subsequently, Dolly's heavily pregnant body elicits the disdainful male gaze of the Rent Collector (p.185), who has clearly made sexist and racist assumptions about Dolly's moral laxity. As is common in patriarchal societies, women are deemed responsible for men's sexual transgressions.

In contrast to the villainous Leon, Errol is the aspiring 'knight in shining armour' (p.187), yet he still performs a kind of male gaze, and his reference to Dolly as 'a lady' complements his heroic self-image. Unsurprisingly, his values and his language reveal an unconscious patriarchal bias. When he first sees Dolly he is captivated by her beauty and he idealises her in a way that verges on dehumanising her. Errol's description of her as a 'living doll' (p.190) utilises an expression that presents women in a sexualised and objectified way.

Wanting to comfort Dolly after the ball, Errol again unthinkingly displays his adherence to patriarchal values when he invites her to become a willing captive in a 'sweet little flat with a ... real stove and a new-fangled Kelvinator' (p.171): in other words, to become one of his possessions. Unlike Leon, Errol has essentially good intentions, but it is clear that his upbringing in a rigidly conservative 1950s domestic environment has shaped his narrow view of the world. It is also clear that Errol has not considered the implications of taking Dolly to the ball in the first place, and thinks that 'what matters' is her, not the fact that she is an Aboriginal woman 'from The Flats' (p.149). What he does not take into account is that Dolly's family is what matters most to her.

Class

Key quote

'A girl from The Flats? I don't even see the town Aboriginals working in stores.' (Nan to Gladys, p.144)

An efficiently functioning society requires a range of occupational roles, assigned on the basis of one's social class, which equip people with appropriate skills and attitudes for future employment. Gladys and Nan are deemed fit only for the hard, physical and badly paid work of fruit and vegetable picking and shiftwork at the cannery, because their lack of education and their identity as Aboriginal Australians effectively disqualify them from better jobs. This ensures that the established social order (which protects the interests of the white middle and upper classes) is not destabilised. Gladys' fight against social determinism drives her quest for Dolly to achieve her 'full potential' (p.134), and it underlies her demands for 'proper schooling' for all her people (p.197).

Dreams and reality

Key quotes

'GLADYS *looks around, fearful that her "daydream" has been witnessed, but it hasn't.*' (p.134)

'They're not really daydreams ...
Because she intends to make them come true.' (Gladys, p.154)

Interrupting the narrative flow of the play are the frequent dream sequences, which offer a comforting escape from (an often unpleasant) reality. Gladys' dream of presenting a bouquet to the Queen, and of being hugged by her, is juxtaposed with the *'bunch of weeds'* she finds herself holding when she comes *'back to reality'* (p.126), having walked a very long way in ill-fitting high heels without catching even a glimpse of the Queen. When the plans for Rumbalara are announced,

Gladys dreams of 'running water', and a tap *'appears from nowhere and from it flows blue jewels in an approximation of water'* (p.155). Gladys' dreams are temporary reprieves from the hardships in her life, but they also allow her to believe that she can *'make them come true'* (p.154). Gladys' fondest dream is to see Dolly as a graduate in an academic cap and gown (p.134). Happily, this dream does seem possible when Dolly is awarded a nursing scholarship (p.191). This miracle might also offer hope for the fulfilment of Gladys' other, seemingly unattainable, dreams – including better housing and career opportunities for her people (p.197).

Dolly, too, slips into a dream world when *'rummaging at the town tip'* (pp.138–9). She visualises a well-groomed salesman courteously offering assistance at a posh store but, in reality, she hoists a roll of discarded lino over her shoulder and walks home from the tip (p.139). Much more poignant is Dolly's dream of winning the 'Miss Mooroopna-Shepparton' title (p.166), which spirals into nightmare when Nancy announces that Dolly's ball gown was made from the discarded curtains her family had dumped at the tip, and the evening becomes a real-life horror scenario when she is raped by Leon (p.172). All ends well, however, with the fairytale finale envisioned in Nan's dream sequence at the end of the play, where there are *'wedding bells and confetti as* DOLLY *and* ERROL ... *get hitched'* (p.198).

DIFFERENT INTERPRETATIONS

Over time, a text will evoke a wide range of responses from its readers, who may come from various social or cultural groups and live in very different places and historical periods. Responses by critics and reviewers can be published in newspapers, journals and books, both online and in print. They can also be expressed in discussions among readers in the media, classrooms, book groups and so on. While there is no single correct reading or interpretation of a text, it is important to understand that an interpretation is more than a personal opinion – it is the justification of a point of view on the text. To present an interpretation of a text based on your point of view, you must use a logical argument and support it with relevant evidence from the text.

The critics' viewpoints

For some critics the play is essentially a compelling human drama. In an uncredited review in *The Age*, the reviewer found a 2005 production directed by Wesley Enoch to fulfil 'expectations of high-quality, thought-provoking and emotionally powerful drama' and argued that 'Harrison's writing is full of subtleties' (*The Age* 2005). ABC critic Kate Munro found the play to be 'a story of strength, family, changing attitudes, defiance, belief and progression' (cited in Encyclopedia.com 2019).

Other reviews focus more on the social, historical and political context being explored by the play. Lynne Lancaster, for example, draws attention to the play's historical setting (1950s Australia), which prompts today's audiences to 'question how much has actually changed ... and whether we can do anything about it'. For Lancaster, the play is about 'one Yorta Yorta family's struggles against assimilation during the Menzies era'. She suggests that, set against the backdrop of the 1954 royal tour, and highlighting the contrast between a British monarch descended from a line of empire-building sovereigns and a family of dispossessed First Nations Australians, the play might make uncomfortable viewing for white audiences – which is certainly part of the playwright's intention. This is evident in her focus on three generations of the Dear family living in a rundown shack on the Goulburn River flats. Audiences witness 'the challenges of being Aboriginal on land colonised by whites and governed by politicians far away'. Lancaster also notes that 'the play has three fabulous, strong parts for women', and concludes by acknowledging the play's depiction of 'Indigenous resilience in the face of ceaseless disadvantage and discrimination', which compels an audience to ask 'what can we do now to right things?' (Lancaster 2019).

Cassie Tongue's 2019 review for timeout.com describes Gladys as 'a bit of a royals tragic' who 'just wants to get a glimpse of the Queen', but the Council has blocked the Queen from the view of First Nations people – and also hidden the humpies along the river from the view of the Queen. Tongue sees *Rainbow's End* as being partly 'about this housing inequality' but 'also about resilience in the face of white supremacy'. Her review, like Lancaster's, emphasises the importance of the three main female characters: 'The women of this play are the smouldering fuel of this production'. Yet she also keeps the play's political aspects in the foreground. Tongue finds that the production, under director Liza-Mare Syron's eye, has been 'staged for clarity' and ensures that 'Harrison's script, and the points it wishes to make, cannot be missed.' Syron, an Indigenous Australian academic, might have brought a degree of intellectual rigour to the production, as well as a strongly feminist stance.

Tongue concludes that 'while the production can veer towards feeling a little formal and presentational, we're never lost'. She sees Gladys' final speech, where she demands 'more from her country and the white systems of power who control it', as 'a rousing call to arms' that 'lands all the harder' because 'we still have so far to go to create an equal nation' (Tongue 2019).

Two Interpretations

Reading 1: Jane Harrison's *Rainbow's End* suggests that there is little hope of a better future for Indigenous Australians.

The family living in the humpy on The Flats represents Indigenous Australians in the mid-twentieth century. They have been driven off their traditional lands; many of their children have been forcibly removed under the Assimilation Policy, as Gladys was, and much of their culture and language has been eliminated in this process. The only hope of a better future lies in education, better paid jobs and suitable career opportunities. While various government agencies ostensibly hold responsibility for ensuring more positive outcomes for Indigenous Australian people, the reality is that nothing changes under a prejudiced and laissez-faire government bureaucracy.

As the play opens, the three strong female characters patch up their humpy after a catastrophic flood, and Gladys invests in a set of encyclopedias to help Dolly reach her 'full potential' (p.134). Gladys is determined that, unlike herself, Dolly will have the opportunity to get a proper job, but Dolly's own ambition is to become a nurse. Because she is doing exceptionally well at school, with grades of As and Bs, she hopes to get a summer job at Trevaks where she might learn to use the cash register, or perhaps obtain a traineeship at the bank where she can use her mathematical skills to become a teller. However, these employment prospects come to nothing. Another hopeful sign is the influence of Papa Dear in the wider community. He is highly respected for doing 'God's work and hard work' (p.143), and he aims to 'make things better for the Aboriginal people' (p.128); yet his travels around the country, and even his meeting with the Queen, do nothing to improve the lives of his people.

Sadly, in 1950s Australia, the play indicates that resilience and determination are not enough to overcome the obstacles facing First Nations Australians. One reason for this is government apathy and inaction and the other is racial discrimination. The government's negligence is revealed in the attitude of the officials who visit the Dear family. The pompous Inspector mentions the importance of 'assimilation' (p.152): a policy designed to eradicate First Nations peoples and their culture. He apparently arranges for Ester's children to be forcibly removed (p.158), irreparably damaging their future prospects.

The Rent Collector criticises their inadequate accommodation, and accuses Nan of 'flouting ... the rules' about the midwife's visiting hours (p.185), aiming to divert attention from the government's neglect of the issue of Aboriginal housing. The Inspector advises the women to 'rally' themselves, placing the onus on the tenants to fix the problems (p.152). First Nations people are also subjected to blatant racial discrimination. The Bank Manager responds to Gladys' request for a traineeship interview for Dolly with a comment that she might not (presumably because of her race) 'fit in' at the bank (p.163). More difficult to challenge is the racism of ordinary white Australians who throw 'stones' at Dolly in the street and make 'snide remarks' (p.162). During the 1950s, such overt racism was commonplace.

One might argue, however, that the ending of the play – with Gladys' inspirational speech and Dolly's nursing scholarship – does provide hope for First Nations Australians' futures. Moreover, Nan's dream of a fairytale wedding for Dolly and Errol (p.198) seems like a traditional happily-ever-after ending to the story. Yet what must also be taken into account is that the play is set in the mid-1950s, and that the writing took place in the early 2000s. As one of the play's reviewers notes, it prompts today's audiences to 'question how much has actually changed ... and whether we can do anything about it' (Lancaster 2019). Disturbingly, this seems to suggest a lack of hope for any imminent change in the lives of First Nations Australians.

Reading 2: *Rainbow's End* suggests that Indigenous Australians can look forward to a better future.

The play opens with Nan and Gladys *'rebuilding after a flood'* (p.123), displaying the kind of stoic resignation that suggests their determination to survive disaster. Their people are thoroughly accustomed to disaster, having survived white civilisation's attempts to rid society of their presence through successive governments' policies of assimilation, which forcibly removed their children and endeavoured to eradicate their culture and language. In fact, the devastating flood itself can be seen as a symbol of colonisation, since their exposure to the rising waters results from their marginalisation on the fringes of the town.

Yet in 1950s Australia, as represented in the play, there are promising signs of change for Indigenous Australian people. The Inspector is familiar with Papa Dear's 'good works' (p.150), and Papa's meeting with the Queen is an acknowledgment of First Nations Australians' rights to be recognised and valued. The assertive women in the Dear family also become agents for political change. Nan refuses to be intimidated by the Rent Collector, who accuses her of 'flouting … the rules' (p.185), and tells him to 'go to blazes' (p.186). This suggests an emergent activism among Indigenous Australians, who will no longer tolerate the racism inherent in government policy and practice.

Gladys also fights for social justice. On the home front, she encourages (perhaps even drives) Dolly's ambition to achieve something more worthy of her intellectual ability than becoming a fruit picker like Nan and Gladys – and many of the other First Nations Australians in her community. Armed with Dolly's impressive school report, Gladys approaches the Bank Manager about a traineeship for a teller's position for Dolly and, surprisingly, he suddenly overcomes his racist sentiments by helping Gladys fill in an application form. Gladys also takes the fight for justice to the male-dominated Shire Council, publicly confronting the councillors with the inappropriateness of their plans to deal with the Aboriginal 'housing problem' (p.181). The negative reaction of the Indigenous community to Gladys' 'radio moment' – they are uncomfortable with her 'drawing attention' to them (p.189) – might indicate how a sense of their perceived racial inferiority could make some First Nations Australians passively accept discriminatory attitudes, but this changes dramatically at the end of the play when Gladys' rousing petition speech is greeted with '*tumultuous applause*' (p.198).

A further sign of hope is evident in Errol's endorsement of First Nations Australians' culture. Thinking he is offering Dolly a 'better life' by suggesting she leave her home and family and move with him to the city (pp.171–2), Errol eventually comes to realise the difference between the materialistic values of white middle-class Australia and the respect for family and community embedded in the idea of home and exemplified by Dolly and her family. It is Errol – in the end – who will leave *his* home and family. Errol's commitment to Dolly and, more importantly, to her culture and her values, is subtly conveyed by his liking for 'snotty googles' (p.191) and his attempt to use Indigenous Australian vernacular.

At the end of the play Gladys' remarkable accomplishment, standing up and reading in public, shows what is possible when individuals are determined to make a difference. Dolly has left behind her pessimism about being able to obtain a good job and has won a nursing scholarship (p.191). Another optimistic sign is Nan's dream sequence of '*wedding bells and confetti*' (p.198) in these final pages, foreshadowing Errol and Dolly's wedding (p.198) and suggesting the possibility of more harmonious relationships between Indigenous and non-Indigenous Australians. The fairytale ending of the play seems to echo the words of the song 'Somewhere Over the Rainbow' from *The Wizard of Oz* (alluded to in the play's title), in which 'dreams really do come true' but, in Harrison's play, this is not through magic but because people like Gladys make it happen.

QUESTIONS & ANSWERS

This section focuses on your own analytical writing on the text, and gives you strategies for producing high-quality responses in your coursework and exam essays.

Essay writing – an overview

An essay on a literary work is a formal and serious piece of writing that presents your point of view on the text, usually in response to a given topic. Your 'point of view' in an essay is your interpretation of the meaning of the text's language, structure, characters, situations and events, supported by detailed analysis of textual evidence.

Analyse – don't summarise

In your essays it is important to avoid simply summarising what happens in a text.

- A **summary** is a description or paraphrase (retelling in different words) of the characters and events. For example: 'Macbeth has a horrifying vision of a dagger dripping with blood before he goes to murder King Duncan.'
- An **analysis** is an explanation of the real meaning or significance that lies 'beneath' the text's words (and images, for a film). For example: 'Macbeth's vision of a bloody dagger shows how deeply uneasy he is about the violent act he is contemplating, and conveys his sense that supernatural forces are impelling him to act.'

A limited amount of summary is sometimes necessary to let your reader know which part of the text you wish to discuss. However, always keep this to a minimum and follow it immediately with your analysis of what this part of the text is really telling us.

Plan your essay

Carefully plan your essay so that you have a clear idea of what you are going to say. The plan ensures that your ideas flow logically, that your argument remains consistent and that you stay on the topic. An essay plan should be a list of **brief dot points** covering no more than half a page.

- Include your central argument or main contention – a concise statement of your overall response to the topic.
- Write three or four dot points for each paragraph, indicating the main idea and evidence/examples from the text. In your essay you will need to *expand* on these points and analyse the evidence.

Structure your essay

An essay is a complete, self-contained piece of writing. It has a clear beginning (the introduction), middle (several body paragraphs) and end (the last paragraph or conclusion). It must also have a central argument that runs throughout, linking each paragraph to form a coherent whole. See examples of introductions and conclusions in the 'Analysing a sample topic' and 'Sample answer' sections.

The introduction establishes your overall response to the topic. It includes your main contention and outlines the main evidence you will refer to in the course of the essay. Write your introduction *after* you have done a plan and *before* you write the rest of the essay.

The body paragraphs argue your case – they present evidence from the text and explain how this evidence supports your argument. Each body paragraph needs:

- a strong topic **sentence** (usually the first sentence) that states the main point being made in the paragraph
- **evidence** from the text, including some brief quotations
- **analysis** of the textual evidence, with **explanation** of its significance and how it supports your argument
- **links back to the topic** in one or more statements, usually towards the end of the paragraph.

Connect the body paragraphs so that your discussion flows smoothly. Use some linking words and phrases such as 'similarly' and 'on the other hand', though don't start every paragraph like this. Another strategy is to use a significant word from the last sentence of one paragraph in the first sentence of the next.

Use key terms from the topic – or synonyms for them – throughout, so the relevance of your discussion to the topic is always clear.

The conclusion ties everything together and finishes the essay. It includes strong statements that emphasise your central argument and provide a clear response to the topic.

Avoid simply restating the points made earlier in the essay – this will end on a very flat note and imply that you have run out of ideas and vocabulary. The conclusion should be a logical extension of what you have written, not just a repetition or summary of it. Writing an effective conclusion can be a challenge. Try using these tips:

- Start by linking back to the final sentence of the second-last paragraph, rather than leaping to your main contention straight away – this helps your writing to flow.
- Use synonyms and expressions with equivalent meanings to vary your vocabulary. This allows you to reinforce your line of argument without being repetitive.
- When planning your essay, think of one or two broad statements or observations about the text's wider meaning. These should be related to the topic and your overall argument. Keep them for the conclusion, since they will give you something 'new' to say but still follow logically from your discussion. The introduction will be focused on the topic, but the conclusion can present a wider view of the text.

Essay topics

1. How does *Rainbow's End* explore ideas about 'the other'?
2. 'Errol's attempt to be "a knight in shining armour" highlights the complexity of being a man in a patriarchal society.' Discuss.
3. 'The characters in *Rainbow's End* are driven by a need for power.' Discuss.
4. '*Rainbow's End* suggests that family relationships can be destructive.' Do you agree?
5. '*Rainbow's End* tells a tragic tale about the loss of culture and identity.' Do you agree?
6. '*Rainbow's End* is a bitter condemnation of colonisation.' Discuss.
7. 'The dream sequences in *Rainbow's End* are the characters' only escape from the depressing reality of life.' Discuss.
8. "A real home is where there are people looking out for each other." How does *Rainbow's End* explore the importance of home?
9. How does the staging of *Rainbow's End* explore the relationships between the characters and their environment?
10. 'Gladys and Dolly are torn between the world of white Australians and their Indigenous Australian heritage.' Discuss.

Vocabulary for writing on *Rainbow's End*

(For further explanation of some of the terms below, refer to the section on 'Genre, structure & language' on pages 10–16 of this guide.)

Allusion: A passing reference to something, carrying an added layer of meaning, is called an allusion. Errol's comment that 'all's well that ends well' (p.137), for example, is an allusion to Shakespeare's play of the same name. This suggests that, like Shakespeare's lovers (whose relationship is problematic), Errol and Dolly will be happily reunited.

Characterisation: Aspects of characters are conveyed through their actions, relationships and dialogue.

Generic feature: The generic features of a drama text include dialogue, stage directions, lighting, costume, props and sound effects. The frequent background sound of radio broadcasts (the royal visit, p.124; *Pick-A-Box*, p.129; the council meeting, p.181), for example, evoke a world of white supremacy and entitlement.

Imagery: A reference to imagery is useful in a discussion of how an idea might be conveyed. The rapturous imagery of Dolly *'swirling and floating'* (p.165) on the dance floor with Errol is contrasted with the dark and menacing imagery of the riverbank, with sound and lighting effects of *'thunder'*, *'lightning'* and *'shadows'*, and a 'sinister voice' nearby (p.172). These graphically convey the vulnerability of women in a patriarchal society that objectifies them.

Irony: Two kinds of irony are verbal irony and situational, or dramatic, irony. Both are evident in *Rainbow's End*. Verbal irony is a feature of Nan's language – for example, in her wry comment that she is 'sure [the cork-tree lads will] want to celebrate the Queen's visit' (p.126). Nan cynically mocks the notion that those who have been most disadvantaged by colonisation might want to 'celebrate' the visit of a member of the empire-building dynasty that seized their lands, murdered their ancestors and crushed their hopes for the future.

Narrative structure: The most obvious structural feature in *Rainbow's End* is the interruption of the narrative by the dream sequences which emphasise a gap between hope and hopelessness for Indigenous Australian characters.

Settings: Discussions of setting should recognise meaningful connections between places and people. Daish's Paddock, the town tip, is one of the proposed sites for the new Aboriginal Housing settlement. The connotations of a tip – as a dumping ground – seem to reflect the white councillors' (and many other white Australians') racist attitudes.

Symbol, symbolism: The place set for Papa Dear at the dinner table (although he hasn't been home for three months) is a symbolic reconnection with him, affirming the importance of the family unit.

Analysing a sample topic

How does *Rainbow's End* explore ideas about 'the other'?

This section outlines an approach to writing an essay in response to the above topic. In general, use the following tips whenever you are analysing a topic and planning a response.

- Read the topic carefully, identifying the word/s and ideas that will be discussed in your response.
- Consult a dictionary for definitions of key words which might have several meanings, and identify those that are relevant.
- Recognise different elements in the topic; be aware that there are likely to be multiple key words (both instruction words and content words) and you need to address all of these, not just one.
- Interrogate the topic – don't simply agree with it. Is the assertion in the topic consistent with what the text tells us?
- Make some preliminary notes identifying textual details that support your interpretation (and note textual details that complicate your argument, and that will need to be resolved).

Sample introduction

> The 'other' is a term describing prejudice against particular groups of people, whose characteristics and customs are used to mark them as separate from accepted social norms, as defined by socially dominant groups. 'Othering' plays a key role in historical patriarchy, where women and non-white minority groups are often deemed inferior, and are exploited and discriminated against. Equally instrumental in reinforcing patriarchal notions of white male superiority is stereotyping, which denies the others' autonomy and individuality. In *Rainbow's End*, Jane Harrison's Indigenous characters are subjected to racism and steroyping, and – if they are female – to misogyny as well.

Body paragraph outline

Paragraph 1

- Racial discrimination creates expectations that the 'otherness' of First Nations Australians makes them inferior. For example, the Bank Manager assumes that Dolly won't 'fit in' at the bank because of her skin colour (p.163), and he endorses a racial stereotype by questioning her capacity for 'reliability' (p.164).
- Also racist is the government Inspector's ridiculous assumption that having white sheets is somehow associated with being white-skinned, and he implicitly emphasises Nan and Gladys' dark-skinned otherness (p.152).
- Racist assumptions are not limited to white characters. Leon accuses Dolly of thinking she is 'too good' to go out with one of her own people (p.167), indicating his own subconscious belief in his (allegedly) unacceptable otherness.
- Leon's angry response to his perceived otherness drastically limits his future prospects. His alcoholism and sexual violence are expressions of his anger at the limitations imposed on him and his community, which his antisocial behaviour will only exacerbate.

Paragraph 2

- When Nancy Woolthorpe humiliates Dolly by announcing that her gown was made from the Woolthorpes' discarded sunroom curtains (p.166), she shows how effectively bullying and exclusion are used in 'othering' those who might threaten the assumed superiority of dominant social groups.
- Errol seems to imply the unacceptable otherness of Dolly's family life when he urges Dolly to move with him to a flat in the city with a 'real stove' and a 'new-fangled Kelvinator' (p.171).
- When Errol repeats his father's notion that his mother has 'funny ideas' about getting a job, he tacitly adheres to middle-class values that unequivocally endorse married, middle-class women's domestic roles and reinforce their dependence on patriarchal power (p.170).

- Unlike Errol, who radically reassesses his middle-class values, compliant characters like his mother are often trapped by patriarchal ideology in lives that are unfulfilling.
- By contrast, Gladys defiantly embraces her otherness. She combines her domestic role with political activism, becoming the voice of her dispossessed people as she publicly confronts race and class discrimination (p.181, pp.196–7).

Paragraph 3

- An effective way of disempowering 'the other' is by reducing people to stereotypes. Errol unthinkingly endorses male gender stereotypes by becoming a 'knight in shining armour' (p.187), attempting to rescue Dolly from poverty and offering her a 'better life' in the city (p.171). In doing so, he not only typecasts her as a helpless female, he categorises her family as the inferior other.
- The Rent Collector's *'disdain'* as he looks at Dolly's *'heavily pregnant'* body (p.185) betrays his sexist assumptions about women's responsibility for men's offensive sexual behaviour.
- Gladys' refusal to accept the limitations imposed on her by a racist, sexist and class-divided society results in *'tumultuous applause'* at the end of her speech (p.198), suggesting that otherness does not necessarily entail inferiority.

Sample conclusion

Rainbow's End shows the harm caused when groups of people are regarded as 'the other', yet it also reveals the importance of personal resilience as well as supportive family structures in providing the strength that individuals need in order to challenge racism and discrimination. Gladys' battle against racial prejudice and patriarchal bias, in particular, and her determination to overcome the limitations of being illiterate, drive her quest for equality for her people. Gladys embraces her otherness and uses it to unite her people as they 'demand to be the equal of anyone'.

SAMPLE ANSWER

"A real home is where there are people looking out for each other." How does *Rainbow's End* reveal the importance of home?

Rainbow's End explores the notion of 'home' through the motif of family relationships. In the play, home can describe a number of concepts, such as a house, sites allocated for Aboriginal housing and the traditional homelands seized by British colonisers. The concept of family includes those living within a household. It also extends to the local Indigenous community and encompasses kinship groups among First Nations people. With its close focus on home and family, the play raises searching questions about what constitutes a 'real home'.

Nan, Gladys and Dolly make their dilapidated humpy as pleasant and comfortable as possible. After a devastating flood, they clean the mud-splattered interior and repair the walls. Dolly finds linoleum at the tip to cover the dirt floor and Gladys retrieves a '*crappy old bookcase*' for the new encyclopedias. In a very practical sense, the women's pride in their domestic environment reflects the importance of the place they call home. A visiting government Inspector remarks on the whiteness of their sheets, and admires Nan's beautifully 'crocheted pillow shams'. Between them, Nan and Gladys also skin rabbits, chop wood, make clothing and use native plants to make nourishing meals when money is short. The women are resourceful and efficient and their humble home becomes a haven: it is aptly described by Dolly as a place where 'there are people looking out for each other'. By contrast, the houses inhabited by Nancy Woolthorpe and Errol, filled with 'new-fangled' consumer goods, seem sterile. The Woolthorpe's 'big fake [Christmas] tree' implies the superficiality of their family values, and Errol's father's insistence on being called 'sir' implies a degree of emotional distance in their relationship, suggesting that they merely occupy houses rather than living in 'real homes'.

Home also refers to areas deemed 'suitable' for 'Aboriginal housing', such as the flood plain or the tip. The Dear family's humpy symbolises the appalling state of Aboriginal housing and exposes an utter lack of concern for First Nations Australians' circumstances by white governments. The new development at Rumbalara is also unsuitable. In forcing Indigenous Australian families to move into *'small, white and featureless'* concrete houses – 'concrete humpies' as Gladys calls them – the Council again fails to provide appropriate housing. Indeed, the white, prefabricated slabs of concrete might also serve as metaphorical representations of the uncaring and inflexible white councillors. The 1954 royal tour presents a particular perspective on the notion of home, with the descendant of an empire-building British monarch enthusiastically welcomed to the land where First Nations Australians were ruthlessly dispossessed. In order to spare the Queen embarrassment, the Aboriginal people's ramshackle dwellings are hidden from royal view.

In the face of hardship and neglect, the Dear women find strength and comfort in loving and mutually supportive relationships. Nan's love for Dolly is expressed by the beautiful ball gown she makes her; in revealing her dark secret about Gladys' real father, Nan reassures Dolly that she, too, can overcome the trauma of sexual assault and 'still love' her child. Nan's trust in her granddaughter strengthens the bond between them and affirms the values that underpin the foundations of a 'real home', while their setting of a place at the dinner table for Papa Dear, who hasn't been home in three months, poignantly highlights their commitment to home and family. Nan and Gladys' relationship is also loving and supportive, despite some tense moments, such as their disagreement over who makes 'the decisions regarding Dolores'. Nan is proud of Gladys' challenge to the councillors: 'My Gladys! Did you hear her?' she exclaims, almost *'hugging the radio'*. Dolly and Gladys clash at times and Dolly occasionally feels pressured by Gladys' determination that she achieve her 'full potential', but she never doubts her mother's love. Furthermore, as the play's fairytale ending suggests, their family relationships are strengthened by being tested, unlike Errol's family, which is ruled by a dogmatic, conservative patriarch. The Dears regard their community as extended family, as shown by their care and concern for Ester and her boys, thus expanding the meaning of 'family' to encompass a wider community of Indigenous Australian people. This is also suggested by Gladys' single-minded pursuit of 'suitable housing', 'proper schooling' and 'jobs in town' for their sons and daughters and her demands for Indigenous people's right to be treated as equals.

The notion of home pervades the play, and what might strongly resonate with theatre audiences are its political ramifications in twenty-first-century Australia regarding First Nations Australians' land rights. Also essential, Gladys insists, is their being 'the equal of anyone', and being 'treated right' by 'neighbours', 'employers', 'the Shire', 'the Crown' and the 'Prime Minister'. More importantly, a humanitarian society unequivocally endorses the notion of social justice and regards a real home as a place where 'townsfolk' don't 'cross the road' to avoid those regarded as 'the other'. It is a requirement, Harrison insists, that is long overdue.

REFERENCES & READING

The text

Harrison, J 2007, *Rainbow's End*, in *Contemporary Indigenous Plays*, Currency Press, Sydney.

References

ABC, Film Victoria & Koorie Heritage Trust Inc. 2004, 'Cummeragunja Mission History', https://web.archive.org/web/20090527022555/http://www.abc.net.au/missionvoices/cummeragunja/mission_history/default.htm

Allam, L & Evershed, N 2019, 'The massacres of Aboriginal people Australia must confront', *The Guardian*, https://www.theguardian.com/australia-news/2019/mar/04/the-killing-times-the-massacres-of-aboriginal-people-australia-must-confront

Atkinson, N 2006, 'The struggle for identity', *The Age*, 2 January, https://www.theage.com.au/national/the-struggle-for-identity-20060102-ge1iel.html

Australian Human Rights Commission 2010, 'Bringing them home – 8. The History – Northern Territory', https://humanrights.gov.au/our-work/bringing-them-home-8-history-northern-territory

Australians Together 2017, 'The importance of land', https://australianstogether.org.au/discover/indigenous-culture/the-importance-of-land/

Casey, M & Craigie, C 2006, 'A brief history of Indigenous Australian contemporary theatre', https://australianplays.org/assets/files/resource/doc/2012/06/BlakStage_Essay_ABriefHistory_DUPL_1.pdf

Edwards, A 2015, 'Jane Harrison: On *Becoming Kirrali Lewis*', *The Garret* podcast, https://thegarretpodcast.com/jane-harrison-on-becoming-kirrali-lewis

Encyclopedia.com 2019, 'Harrison, Jane 1960–', https://www.encyclopedia.com/arts/educational-magazines/harrison-jane-1960

'Jane Harrison' 2019, AustLit, https://www.austlit.edu.au/austlit/page/A34457

Lancaster, L 2019, 'Review: Rainbow's End, Darlinghurst Theatre (NSW)' ArtsHub, https://www.artshub.com.au/news/reviews/review-rainbows-end-darlinghurst-theatre-nsw-258611-2364225/

Lehman, N 2015, 'Q&A with Jane Harrison, author of Becoming Kirrali Lewis', Readings, https://www.readings.com.au/news/qanda-with-jane-harrison-author-of-becoming-kirrali-lewis

Reconciliation Australia 2020, '2020 Australian Reconciliation Barometer', https://www.reconciliation.org.au/wp-content/uploads/2021/02/Australian_Reconciliation_Barometer_-2020_Summary-Report_web_spread.pdf

River Connect 2011, 'The Flats', https://riverconnect.com.au/education/culture/theflats

The Age 2005, 'Rainbow's End', https://www.theage.com.au/entertainment/art-and-design/rainbows-end-20050222-gdzn5t.html

Tongue, C 2019, 'Rainbow's End review', *TimeOut*, https://www.timeout.com/sydney/theatre/rainbows-end-review